SPINNING AND DYEING YARN

First edition for North America and the Philippines
published in 2014 by Barron's Educational Series, Inc.

© 2013 RotoVision SA, Sheridan House
114 Western Road, Hove
East Sussex BN3 1DD
UK

All inquiries should be addressed to:
Barron's Educational Series, Inc.
250 Wireless Boulevard
Hauppauge, New York 11788
www.barronseduc.com

ISBN: 978-0-7641-6607-5

Library of Congress Control No. 2013935753

Commissioning Editor: Isheeta Mustafi
Art Director: Emily Portnoi
Art Editor: Jennifer Osborne
Design concept: Katy Abbott
Layout: Rebecca Stephenson and Jennifer Osborne
Cover Design: Emily Portnoi
Tutorial photography: Sarah Robbins
All other photography: Michael Wicks

Credits
Page 50: Handcrafted hackle by Blue Mountain
Handcrafts: www.bluemountainhandcrafts.com
Page 136: Wirespun yarns by Melissa Nasby
Page 138: Corespun yarn from Border Leicester locks
Pages 150/151: Art bouclé yarn by Melissa Yoder Ricks

Printed in China

9 8 7 6 5 4 3 2 1

SAFETY NOTE:
For the purposes of clarity in the step-by-step
photographs, the author did not wear gloves for the
tutorials included in this book. Please note that it is good
practice to wear gloves to protect your hands when you
are using equipment that has spikes or abrasive surfaces.

We used non-toxic dyes for the tutorials photographed
for this book. Non-toxic dyes don't require the protection
of gloves or face masks. For dyeing wool, food colorings
provide an excellent non-toxic option. Good sources
are colorings used for cakes and cake frostings, and
Kool-Aid powders.

However, most commercial dyes contain heavy metals.
When you work with such dyes, you must wear gloves
and work in a well-ventilated area. You should always
wear gloves and a mask when working with powdered
commercial dyes. Never use the same equipment for
dyeing and food preparation; keep all the equipment
you use for dyeing yarns separate from your kitchen
equipment. And for any dye, always follow the safety
instructions on the manufacturer's label.

SPINNING AND DYEING YARN

The Home Spinner's Guide to Creating
Traditional and Art Yarns

ASHLEY MARTINEAU

BARRON'S

Contents

Foreword   6

Section One
Fiber Identification and Preparation   8

Chapter 1: Types of Fiber   **10**
Fine Wool   12
Medium Wool   13
Coarse Wool   14
Longwool   15
Alpaca and Llama   16
Goat   17
Rabbit   18
Silk   19
Plant   20
Synthetic   21

Chapter 2: Washing Fiber   **22**
Buying Raw Wool   24
Skirting Wool   25
Washing Wool   26
Building a Drying Rack   28
Caring for Wool   30

Chapter 3: Preparing Fiber   **32**
Equipment   34
Processing Methods   36
Worsted vs. Woolen   37
Hand Picking Wool   38
Using a Picker   39
Combing Wool   40
Using Hand Carders   42
Blending on a Drum Carder   44
Carding Art Batts on a Drum Carder   46
Building a Hackle   48
Dizzing from a Hackle   50

GALLERY: Batts and Dizzed Fibers   52
PROFILE: Tina Watson   58

Section Two
Dyeing Techniques   60

Chapter 4: Dyeing Fiber   **62**
Animal Fiber   64
Plant Fiber   66
Synthetic Fiber   67
Immersion Dyeing   68
Gradient Dyeing   70
Hand Painting   72
Solar Dyeing   74
Tie Dyeing   76

GALLERY: Dyed Fibers   78
PROFILE: Lexi Boeger   82

Section Three
Spinning Techniques   84

Chapter 5: Drop Spindles   **86**
Choosing a Drop Spindle   88
Building a Drop Spindle   90
Spinning   92
Corespinning   94
Plying   95

Chapter 6: Kick Spindles   **96**
Building a Kick Spindle   98
Spinning   100
Corespinning   102
Plying   103
Fancy Plying   104
Thread Wrapping   106
Mixed Media: Spinning Beads into a Single   108
Mixed Media: Plying Beads into a Single   110

GALLERY: Drop Spun Yarns   112
PROFILE: Michelle Snowdon   118

Chapter 7: Spinning Wheels   **120**
Choosing a Spinning Wheel   122
Building a Spinning Wheel   124
Spinning a Thick and Thin Single   132
Spinning Locks   134
Corespinning Wire   136
Corespinning Batts   137
Fancy Corespinning   138
Corespinning Locks   140
Thread Wrapping   141
Plying Basics   142
Plying Bubbles   144
Plying Coils   145
Plying Shells   146
Plying Cocoons   148
Navajo Plying   149
Art Bouclé   150
Sluggy Plying   152
Recycled Yarn   154
Mixed Media: Corespinning   156
Mixed Media: Plying   157
Mixed Media: Single Ply   158
Mixed Media: Fabric   159

Chapter 8: Setting the Twist   **160**
Setting Traditional Yarns   162
Setting Art Yarns   164
Building a Niddy Noddy   166
Using a Niddy Noddy   167
Alive Yarns   168

GALLERY: Handspun Yarns   170
PROFILE: Ruru Mori   176

Section Four
Going Professional   178

Chapter 9: Developing a Brand   **180**
Inspiration   182
Photography   184
Building a Lightbox   186
Vending Tips   188
Selling Online   190
Shipping and Handling   192

Resources   194
Useful Websites   196
Further Reading   197
Glossary   198
Contributors   200
Index   204
Acknowledgments   208

Foreword

A number of years ago, stepping into the edge of the world of handspinning, I felt as if I had stumbled across a magical, secret garden that had been hiding in plain sight of me. Like so many before me, I was completely captivated by the feeling of wanting to make beautiful yarn, but was starting from a place of complete ignorance.

Not only did I not understand how to go about learning, I also had no idea about the depth of knowledge involved in creating yarn. In response to my desire, I haphazardly went about choosing my first wheel, buying books, and accumulating fiber and knowhow. Slowly, things started coming together.

Contrast my path to the one I might have taken a few hundred years ago, when learning to spin might well have been part of my routine acquisition of necessary life skills as a woman—but this is not so anymore. However, while the oral tradition of passing knowledge down the generations has fallen by the wayside, one can now quickly access the necessary resources via the Internet—websites and social networking, books, videos, clubs, and classes. I went from having no information at all to being completely overwhelmed by what was available.

But where was the resource that could have simplified this learning process for me? Where was the resource that could have pointed me toward the inspiring and helpful community that was waiting to be discovered? Where was the helpfully gathered information that could explain the basics of building my fiber arts practice into a business, if that's what I wanted to do?

You are now holding that resource in your hands. This book sets you on the right path from the outset. Follow the advice contained in these pages and you will be able to access the practical knowledge you need right away. I wish this book had been available to me as an aspiring spinner, and am excited now to have it as one of my "go to" reference works.

Through my experience as publisher of www.spinartiste.com, I have the pleasure of getting to know many talented and brilliant artists. The author of this work, Ashley Martineau, is certainly a member of that group. Beyond that, Ashley believes in helping to build her community. This book is an extension of Ashley's generous nature, and many thanks go to her for so graciously sharing her wisdom and experience!

Best,

Arlene Ciroula, publisher
www.spinartiste.com

Opposite: Yarn spun by Brittany Wilson

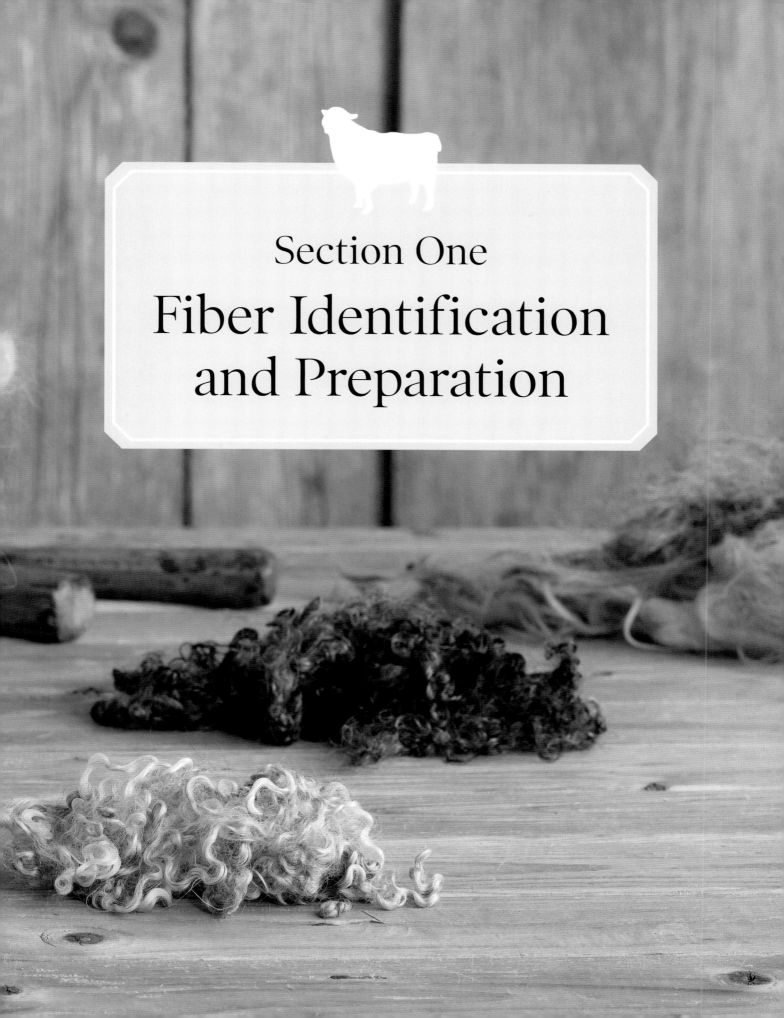

Section One
Fiber Identification and Preparation

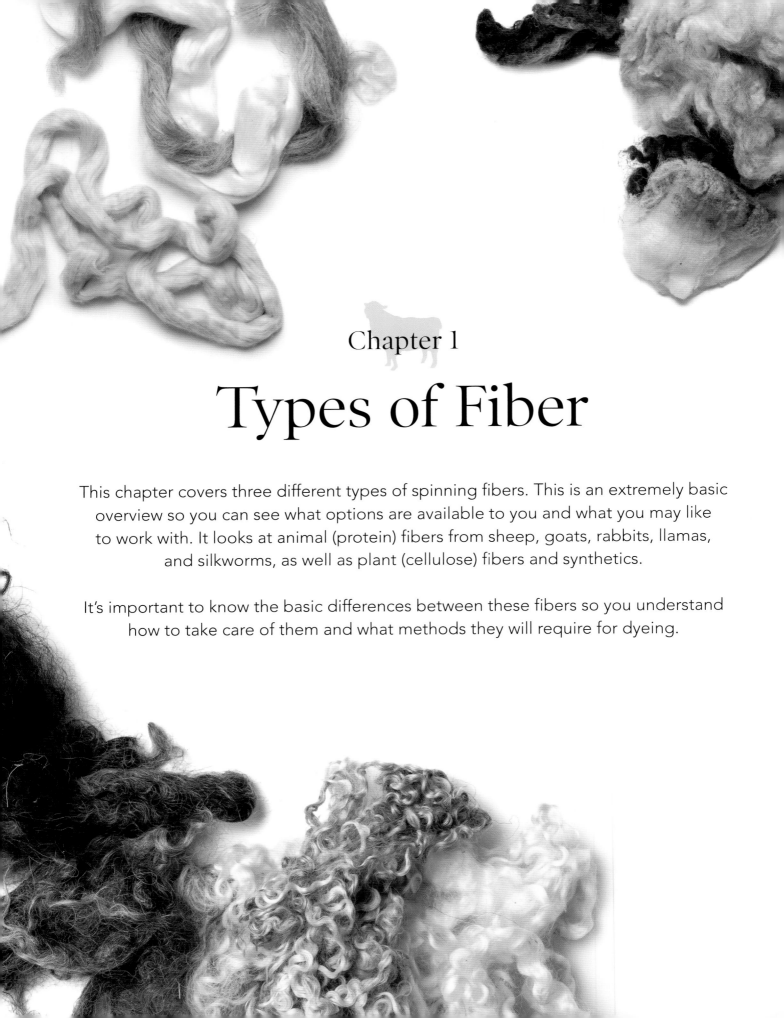

Chapter 1

Types of Fiber

This chapter covers three different types of spinning fibers. This is an extremely basic overview so you can see what options are available to you and what you may like to work with. It looks at animal (protein) fibers from sheep, goats, rabbits, llamas, and silkworms, as well as plant (cellulose) fibers and synthetics.

It's important to know the basic differences between these fibers so you understand how to take care of them and what methods they will require for dyeing.

Opposite, clockwise from top left: Commercially processed top (cotton, silk, and flax); a mixture of various breeds of raw wools; raw wool (coarse, medium, and long), ready to be washed
Top: Various textures and natural colors of fiber
Above: Curly Wensleydale locks in natural gray

Troubleshooting Tips

Problem: I received a "mystery fleece" and don't know what breed of sheep it is from. Is there any way of finding out just by looking at the wool?
Solution: There isn't a trustworthy way of identifying the specific breed of sheep that your wool came from without speaking to the farmer who raised the animal, but you can identify it as fine/medium/long/coarse based on the texture characteristics described in this chapter.

Problem: I want to spin yarn but I am allergic to wool. What are my options?
Solution: Try alpaca, which is hypoallergenic. If that bothers your allergies, consider spinning plant fibers or silks. You can also spin synthetic fibers (nylon), such as faux cashmere, faux angora, and faux mohair.

Problem: I find most wools to be itchy and irritating. What are my options?
Solution: First, don't discount all wools. Try spinning a superfine Merino top, or a Merino/silk blend. There are many commercial fiber blends that still include wool and are next-to-skin soft. If any wool blend bothers you, try a blend with alpaca. Most commercial tops blended with silk are very soft.

Problem: What are my options for spinning fiber into yarn that is machine washable?
Solution: Superwash wools have been processed to remove the scales that cause the fibers to felt. Superwash yarns can be knitted, crocheted, or woven into items that can be washed in a commercial washing machine. Use a gentle cycle for machine washing handspun yarns, and always wash these yarns with delicates.

Fine Wool

Fine wool is the most popular choice for spinning, because of its softness. The most common fine wool breeds are Cormo, Merino, Polwarth, Debouillet, Rambouillet, and various crosses. The finer and softer the wool, the slower it grows on the sheep. Therefore, when shopping for raw fine wool fleeces, look for a staple length of at least 2 inches (5 cm) for easy spinning.

Fine wool is perfect for spinning into yarns for wearing next to the skin, or for snuggling. Sweaters, socks, mittens, scarves, hats, baby items, and blankets are all popular projects for making use of fine wool yarns.

To increase softness, fine wools are blended with luxury fibers such as silk and alpaca. Fine wools are also perfect for carding into batts (see pages 42–47). Blending fine wool with nylon increases its durability.

Fine wool is the most delicate wool, and felts easily with heat and agitation. Even storing fine wool in plastic can cause it to felt (see "Caring for Wool" on page 30). Be extra gentle when washing and dyeing fine wool to prevent felting.

From top to bottom: Merino/silk blend processed top, washed Merino, washed Cormo, raw (unwashed) Merino

Fine wool	Relative cost
Cormo	$$$
Merino	$$$
Polwarth	$$
Debouillet	$$
Rambouillet	$$

Medium Wool

Medium wool is often the most affordable spinning wool. The most common medium wool breeds are Cheviot, Columbia, Corriedale, Dorset, Oxford, Perendale, Romney, Southdown, Shetland, Shropshire, Targhee, and various crosses. Medium wool sheep are usually sheared in the spring and fall. The wool grows quickly and often has a staple length of over 3 inches (7.5 cm). Medium wool is easy to spin and does not felt as easily as fine wool. It is perfect for beginning spinners and dyers.

Medium wool can be used for spinning into yarns soft enough for wearing next to the skin that also require some durability. Sweaters, mittens, scarves, and hats are all popular projects that make use of medium wool yarns.

Medium wool comes in countless natural colors ranging from white to gray, tan, brown, and black. The highest quality medium wool fleeces can be as soft as some fine wool fleeces. The softness of the fleece also depends on the quality of care the sheep receives, and not merely the classification of the breed.

Medium wool	Relative cost
Cheviot	$
Columbia	$
Corriedale	$
Dorset	$
Oxford	$
Perendale	$
Romney	$
Southdown	$
Shetland	$$
Shropshire	$
Targhee	$

From top to bottom: Raw Shetland, washed Merino/Romney cross, raw Romney wool

Coarse Wool

Coarse wool comes from sheep known as primitive breeds. They have a dual-coated fleece: a long, hairlike overcoat and a short, downy undercoat. The long, hairy overcoat can often reach a length of over 7 inches (18 cm). This unique wool protects them from the elements. Coarse wool breeds include Icelandic, Karakul, Navajo churro, Scottish blackface, and various crosses.

Coarse wool is also referred to as "carpet wool" and is traditionally used to make rugs, because of its superior durability. Coarse wool comes in countless natural colors ranging from white to gray, tan, brown, and black. The softness of the fleece also depends on the quality of care the sheep receives, and not merely the classification of the breed.

From top to bottom: Navajo churro, gray Icelandic, white Icelandic, brown Icelandic

Coarse wool	Relative cost
Icelandic	$
Karakul	$
Navajo churro	$
Scottish blackface	$

Longwool

Longwool sheep are often sheared twice a year because their fleeces grow so quickly. Some shepherds shear their longwool sheep once a year, and many spinners pay top dollar for those unique 12-inch (30-cm) or longer fleeces. Longwool breeds include Leicester, Coopworth, Cotswold, Lincoln, Perendale, Romney, Teeswater, Wensleydale, and various crosses.

Longwool is a lustrous, curly wool that is very popular among spinners. It comes in many natural colors including white, gray, brown, and black. It is easy to spin and makes beautiful textured yarns. Many spinners use longwool yarns to embellish the cuffs of mittens and hats. Some spinners enjoy making pillows and purses out of textured longwool yarns.

The highest quality longwool fleeces can be as soft as some medium wool fleeces. The softness of the fleece also depends on the quality of care the sheep receives, and not merely the classification of the breed.

From top to bottom: Locks of Border Leicester, Lincoln, Cotswold, Wensleydale

Longwool	Relative cost
Leicester	$$
Coopworth	$
Cotswold	$$
Lincoln	$$
Perendale	$
Romney	$
Teeswater	$$$
Wensleydale	$$$

Alpaca and Llama

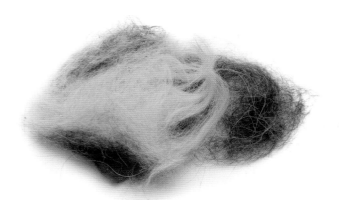

The difference between alpaca and llama fiber is that llama has two distinct coats: an overcoat of guard hair and an undercoat of soft billowy fiber. Alpacas have guard hair, but far less than llamas. Many spinners will send their llama fiber to mills to remove the guard hair.

Alpacas produce soft and strong fiber that requires minimal processing before spinning. It is easy to clean, and many spinners enjoy spinning it raw (before washing) because it does not contain as much grease and oil as raw sheep's wool.

There are two breeds of alpaca: suri and huacaya. Suri is lustrous and slippery, and often falls in locks with a curly tip. Suri alpacas are usually shorn every two years. Huacaya is crimpy and billowy, and can be as soft as cashmere. Huacaya alpacas are shorn every year. Llama fiber is usually separated into three categories: light wool, heavy wool, and silky.

Alpaca and llama fibers are hypoallergenic and come in over 20 different natural colors, ranging from deep auburns to grays, blacks, browns, whites, and shades of peach.

From top to bottom: Suri alpaca, llama wool, a mix of alpaca wools

Alpaca and llama	Relative cost
Suri alpaca	$$
Huacaya alpaca	$$
Llama (light wool)	$
Llama (heavy wool)	$
Llama (silky)	$$

Goat

There are three different types of goats that produce fiber for spinning: cashmere, angora, and pygora. Cashmere goats grow the highest quality cashmere fiber on their bellies. This fiber also includes a large amount of guard hair, which must be removed by a mill before spinning. Cashmere is one of the softest and most luxurious fibers in the world.

Angora goats grow mohair: a luxurious fiber very popular among spinners. It is known for its luster, silkiness, and strength. A quality mohair fleece will have a curly staple length of at least 4 inches (10 cm). Angora goats can grow 1 inch (2.5 cm) of fiber per month, and are usually shorn twice a year.

Pygora goats are a crossbreed between a pygmy and an angora goat. The fiber from a pygora goat can range from shiny 6-inch (15-cm) ringlets, to fine fiberlike cashmere. Many spinners use pygora for lace and shawls.

Mohair and pygora can be very greasy when raw, but a water temperature over 160°F (70°C) and commercial-grade scouring liquid will clean this fiber well (see pages 26–27).

Above: Natural mohair locks

Goat	Relative cost
Cashmere	$$$
Angora	$$
Pygora	$$

Rabbit

There are five different types of Angora rabbits: English, French, Satin, German, and Giant. Each type of Angora rabbit produces a different quantity, quality, and color range of fiber. Angora fiber is known for its softness and its "halo" of delicate fluff around the yarn. Angora comes in many natural colors, including white, tan, gray, brown, and black.

Angora rabbits are either plucked (loose fibers are gently removed) or sheared. Plucked fibers generally have less guard hair, but the process is slow and tedious. Some Angora breeders prefer to shear (cut) the fiber from the rabbit, which takes less time and results in more fiber (although more guard hairs are included).

Angora is such a fine, delicate fiber that it tends to felt easily. Therefore many spinners will blend angora with other soft fibers, such as alpaca or cashmere, to achieve the "halo" effect without felting. Angora can also be blended with fine wool such as Merino to improve elasticity. Once spun, these fiber blends make beautiful sweaters, accessories, and embellishments.

Rabbit	Relative cost
English	$$
French	$$
Satin	$$$
German	$$
Giant	$$

Above: Naturally colored Angora rabbit fiber

Silk

Before a silkworm becomes a moth, it makes a cocoon of silk around itself. Silk comes in many different forms: cocoons, noils, caps, combed top (just to name a few). Cocoons have the dead silkworm inside and require processing before spinning. Silk noils are great for carding into batts (see pages 42–47), and silk hankies are a popular fiber for spinning on a drop spindle. Many spinners enjoy spinning silk top into a smooth and superfine yarn for knitting or crochet.

There are two kinds of silk top. Mulberry silk top is usually pure white and very shiny, and is made from cultivated silkworms fed a strict diet of mulberry leaves. Tussah silk is less shiny and slick, and has a honey color. It comes from silkworms that eat a varied mulberry plant diet.

Silk is known for its shine and luxurious softness. It is the thinnest and warmest of all animal fibers, and yet very durable. Many spinners blend silk with wool and alpaca to add shine, softness, and strength. Silk can be dyed using the same methods as for dyeing wool (see pages 64–65).

From top to bottom: Mulberry silk cocoons, natural gold silk cocoons, processed mulberry silk top, silk noils, a silk hankie (mawata)

Silk	Relative cost
Cocoons	$
Noils	$
Mulberry (white) top	$$$
Hankies	$$$
Tussah (honey) top	$$

Plant

Plant fibers are also called cellulose fibers. The most popular types are cotton, flax, and hemp. They are light and breathable, perfect for spinning yarns for summer projects.

Cotton can be found as loose fiber or cotton top. It has a much shorter staple length than wool, and is more challenging to spin. Beginner spinners should try spinning cotton top before loose cotton fiber. You will need a spinning wheel with a high ratio to spin cotton.

Yarn spun from flax is called linen—one of the oldest spinning fibers. It is stronger than cotton and has a high natural luster. Many weavers prefer linen as their warp thread because of its strength. Spinning wet flax (rather than dry) activates the pectin in the fiber, which results in a very strong and smooth yarn. Flax is traditionally used as single-spun yarn.

Hemp can be spun like flax, but it is not as smooth as flax. It is a versatile fiber that is also ecofriendly and is growing in popularity among handspinners.

Plant fibers require a unique dyeing process (see page 66).

From top to bottom: Flax top, cotton top, loose cotton fiber

Plant	Relative cost
Cotton (loose)	$
Cotton (top)	$$
Flax (top)	$
Hemp (top)	$

Synthetic

Synthetic fibers are manufactured by melting a polymer and then extruding it through a spinneret. The fiber then solidifies by cooling, evaporating, or a chemical reaction. Synthetic fibers include Angelina and various forms of nylon, including Firestar and faux versions of mohair, cashmere, and angora.

Synthetic fibers such as Angelina and Firestar are often blended with natural fibers to give them sparkle, shine, and glitz. Some spinners use nylon "faux" fibers if they are allergic to animal fibers.

Synthetic fibers made from nylon can be dyed using the same methods as for dyeing wool (see pages 64–65).

Angelina is growing in popularity and comes in various lengths and textures. Many spinners prefer Angelina that is 8 inches (20 cm) long without crimp, because it is the smoothest and silkiest. It is a favorite for carding into art batts (see pages 46–47).

From top to bottom: Gold Angelina, faux cashmere, Firestar, nylon fiber

Synthetic	Relative cost
Angelina	$$$
Firestar	$
Faux fibers (nylon)	$

Chapter 2

Washing Fiber

Washing fiber correctly will help keep your fiber processing equipment clean and your fibers from getting damaged. Heat and agitation are the two biggest factors that cause felting of animal fibers. By eliminating these, you will be able to process your own locally grown farm-fresh fleeces in your home. This chapter covers the basics of wool washing in small and large loads, as well as how to store your clean wool to protect it from moths and how to properly dry your fiber so it isn't susceptible to mildew.

Opposite, clockwise from top left: Soaking raw wool in hot, soapy water removes the grease (lanolin) from the fiber for easy spinning; raw white wool often has a yellow appearance due to the grease (lanolin) in the fiber; every sheep is different, and fleeces vary from year to year—lamb fleeces often have a tight curly tip (white wool, right) and adult fleeces tend to have a more uniform texture (gray fleece, left)
Top: Try putting raw wool in mesh laundry bags to prevent wool from clogging your drain
Bottom: Spinning the water from wet wool will speed up the drying process—you can use a salad spinner for smaller loads, or a spin dryer for larger loads

Troubleshooting Tips

Problem: I keep soaking my fiber in hot, soapy water and it isn't getting clean.
Solution: Try increasing the heat of the water (to 160–170°F/70–78°C). It's possible that you have too much fiber in the water. Try washing less wool at a time, with a higher-quality soap, and hotter water. Fine sheep's wool takes more time to wash than medium or coarse wools. Often very fine wools such as alpaca, llama, and angora can be washed after spinning. Mohair and goat fibers often need hotter water and stronger soap to remove the grease.

Problem: After I washed my fiber I cannot pull it apart; it's stuck together in clumps.
Solution: Unfortunately you have felted your fiber. This was caused by agitation while the fiber was being washed, and by temperature changes. Any time you place hot fiber in cool water it will be prone to felting. Make sure every hot water bath you use is hotter than the soapy fiber, and avoid agitation.

Problem: My fiber has a moldy odor after drying.
Solution: Your fiber took too long to dry, or patches remained damp during the drying process. Re-wash the fiber and add some white vinegar to the final rinse water. Then lay the fiber out to dry on your drying rack, less than 1 inch (2.5 cm) thick across. Place a couple of fans on the fiber to speed up the drying process so that it dries before it mildews. Every couple of hours rotate the fiber so the damp underside also has a chance to dry quickly. In damp climates, your fiber should be dry within 48 hours. In warm climates the fiber will dry in an afternoon.

Problem: I thought my fiber was clean, but after it dried it feels tacky.
Solution: This often happens with fine wool fibers such as Merino. Begin the washing process again. If the water has a milky white appearance in your soapy hot water soaks, that is grease coming off the fiber. Continue with hot water and soap soaks until the water runs completely clear. Then rinse your fiber in hot water and lay it out to dry.

Buying Raw Wool

The first step in selecting a fleece is to decide what type of project you have in mind. Do you want a fine fiber for a next-to-the-skin item, or a durable fiber for outerwear? Do you want a fine wool, coarse wool, longwool, a camelid, or a goat fleece?

Once you decide on a fiber type, it is time to find a farm. Many breeders are listed on specific breed association websites, which you can find easily by searching on the Internet. There are many online sources and social networks for spinners looking for fleece. Ravelry (www.ravelry.com) is a great place to search for fleeces and network with other spinners.

There are certain things you need to consider when buying a fleece.

- Was the animal coated?
- How much vegetable matter is in the fleece?
- How many second cuts are there?
- What is the lock strength?

Animal coats

A coat is a thin, breathable jacket the animal wears to keep vegetable matter (hay, straw, twigs) out of the fleece. Be sure to ask if the animal was coated year-round or for only part of the year. If it was only coated for part of the year, ask how much vegetable matter is present in the fleece.

Vegetable matter

Some shepherds have pristine grass pastures and don't feed their animals hay. Snow and rain naturally keep the fleeces very clean. However, sheep tend to eat hay over their neighbors' backs at the feeder. Fleeces that contain lots of vegetable matter will take extra effort and time to process.

Second cuts

Second cuts are caused when the shear does not come close enough to the skin, and a second cut is taken to get the rest of the wool off. Avoid a fleece with excessive second cuts.

Lock strength

Ask the shepherd for a lock of wool. Pull off a pencil-sized diameter of wool from the lock. Pull on the fiber with a gentle yet firm tug to check for brittleness and breaks. Fiber that breaks may indicate that the animal was sick or stressed. It is not recommended to buy a fleece with breaks.

If you have additional questions about a fleece, ask the shepherd. They should be willing to help you select a fleece and answer your questions.

Above: Raw fine wool fleece from Herman Hills Farm

Skirting Wool

Skirting wool is when you separate good wool from bad wool. Many fleeces you find at farms and fiber fairs are already skirted. When buying raw wool, ask the farmer if the wool has been skirted.

Good wool is clean, long-stapled, and has the best texture in the fleece. Bad wool is dirty, has too much vegetable matter (hay, sticks, grass), and is matted or undesirable for spinning.

Spread your fleece out as it was sheared from the sheep. A good shearer will have the fleece wrapped into a bag in such a way that you can unroll it like a blanket. Place the sheared side down with the tips of the wool facing up—just as it was on the sheep.

Begin skirting by removing any wool with dung tags or britch. The britch wool is from the legs and belly of the sheep and has a coarser texture than the wool from the back and shoulders. All of this dirty wool can be thrown away or used as compost.

Also remove any parts of the wool that contain too much vegetable matter. Remove any matts or burrs or second cuts you may find. The more skirting you do, the easier it will be to wash and prepare the fiber. Many spinners prefer their fleeces "heavily skirted," and go by the motto, "When in doubt, throw it out!"

Above: A selection of wool ready to be skirted

Washing Wool

Use the hottest water possible. If you don't have access to a hot water heater, start boiling some water on the stove as a backup to keep the temperature of the wash water hot. You can also wash an entire fleece in a top-loading washing machine, but make sure it has first been heavily skirted.

1 Begin by filling up one of the plastic tubs or the bathtub with hot (160°F/70°C) water. Once the tub has been filled, add soap to the water. (Try a high-quality degreasing dish soap.) Make sure the soap you are using does not have bleach or "oxy" additives, as these will damage the wool fibers. Add enough soap to the water so that the water feels slimy to the touch. Then add the wool, in the mesh bag. As the wool sinks into the water, the water will turn a brown color as the oil immediately dissolves off the fiber. Don't overfill the tub with wool.

2 Allow the wool to sit in the tub for 15 minutes. Take the temperature every 5 minutes to make sure the water temperature does not fall below 140°F (60°C). Add hot water from the stove to increase the temperature of the wash if necessary, but do not pour it directly onto the wool.

+
If your fleece is excessively dirty (dusty or greasy, or both), soak it overnight in cold water to help release some of the dirt. Soaking wool will not remove vegetable matter, but it will help loosen the dirt from the locks before washing.

Materials

Raw wool fleece (heavily skirted) | Liquid dish soap | Hot water
Mesh laundry bags (optional) | For large loads: bathtub or large plastic bin
For small loads: sink or small plastic bin

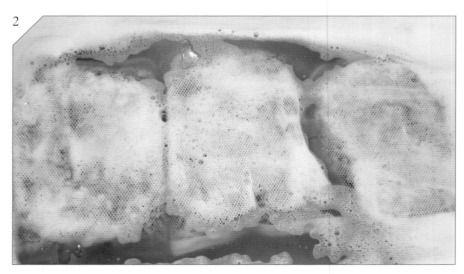

3 After 15 minutes of soaking, pull the wool bag out of the tub and pour out the dirty soapy water. Then begin filling the tub again with hot (160°F/70°C) water. Make sure the temperature of the water is always hotter than the wool you are adding to it to prevent felting.

4 Place the wool bag in the tub of hot water. If the water of your second wash is still dirty (tan in color) lift the wool out and add soap to the water and place the strainer of wool back into the tub. Let the wool sit in this soapy water for another 15 minutes (keep an eye on the temperature), then lift it out of the tub, pour out the water and refill the tub with hot water, and add the wool back into the hot water. Continue with soapy water soaks until you add the strainer of wool to the hot water and it remains clear. This is your final rinse. Allow the wool to soak for 10 minutes and pull it out of the hot water. Then gently place the wool on your drying rack and spread it out to air dry. You can see examples of washed locks below.

3

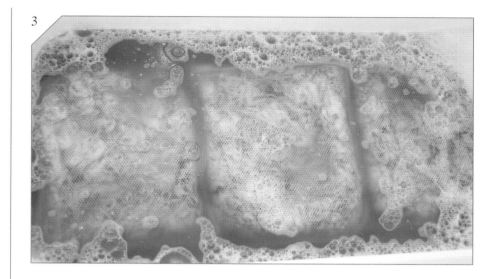

4

Building a Drying Rack

This drying rack is a perfect addition to your home studio if you will be doing a lot of wool washing or dyeing. You can alter the dimensions to fit into a corner of your studio, and add as many height levels as you need. When you aren't using the drying rack, simply remove the legs and safely store it away.

1 Take four of the 2-foot (60-cm) pieces of PVC pipe and attach the four-way corner joints to create a square. After you have created all of the squares you need for the drying rack, attach the 6-inch (15-cm) PVC pipe legs.

2 Cut a piece of the plastic garden mesh 3 inches (7.5 cm) larger than each square of the drying rack.

+ You can build this drying rack to any dimensions that will suit your fiber drying needs. You can also use recycled wood instead of PVC pipe for the frame.

Materials

For each level: 4 × 2-foot (61-cm) sections of ½-inch (1.25-cm) PVC pipe | 4½-inch (11.4-cm) PVC four-way corner joints | 4 × 6-inch (15.2-cm) sections of ½-inch (1.25-cm) PVC pipe for the legs | 1 × PVC four-way joint | Plastic garden mesh netting | Zip ties

1

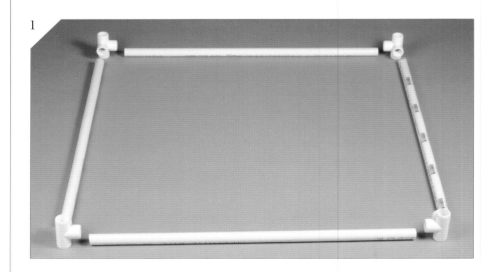

2

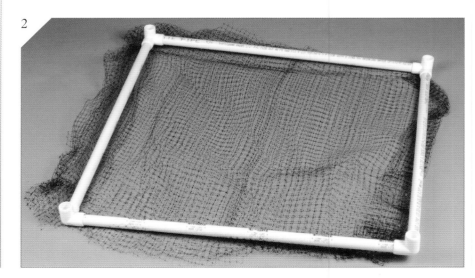

3 Attach the garden mesh with zip ties and cut the ends.

4 Once you have assembled all the layers of your drying rack, you can stack them on top of one another by putting the 6-inch (15-cm) PVC pipe legs into each of the four-way corner joints.

5 Now your drying rack is ready to use. After washing your wool (see pages 26–27) you can spread it out on the drying rack to air dry over a couple of days. You can also dry your dyed wool on this rack. Since this rack is made of plastic, you can place it outside in the sun without it warping or getting damaged. In moist climates, place a box fan or two facing the wool to speed up the drying process.

3
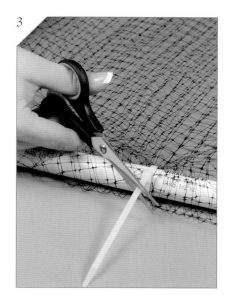

4
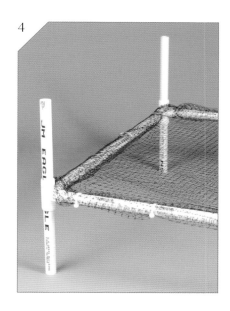

5

Caring for Wool

Drying Wool

Wool can hold up to 30 percent of its weight in water without feeling damp. In order to prevent your wool from becoming musty, it is very important to dry it thoroughly and keep it dry after washing or dyeing it.

Some spinners like to use a spin dryer or a salad spinner to remove excess water from their wool before putting it on the drying rack. You can order spin dryers in various sizes online. When you place the wool on your drying rack, spread it out so that it has room to breathe. You can place a box fan near your drying rack to speed up the drying process.

Seasonal and climatic changes can affect how quickly your wool dries. Wet wool will dry in an afternoon in full sun in a dry climate. But in a cool, damp climate it is best to use a fan on the wool and rotate it every few hours as you wait for it to dry.

If your wool feels cool to the touch, it is still damp. Continue allowing your wool to dry until it no longer feels cool to the touch.

Storing Clean Wool

If wool is stored in plastic bags, it may sweat and mildew, or even felt. It is recommended to use old cotton pillowcases to store wool. Some farmers prefer using burlap bags.

Fill a cotton pillowcase or burlap bag with the clean, thoroughly dry wool. You can then place this cotton pillowcase in an airtight plastic container to prevent moth infestation. Including a lavender sachet or cedar block in each pillowcase is also a sweet-scented way to deter moths.

Top: Sachets of cedar help prevent moth infestations
Bottom: Using a spin dryer or salad spinner to remove water from your wool after it has been washed will speed up the drying process
Opposite: Storing wool in a clean, moth-free environment will keep it dry and sweet-smelling for years to come

Chapter 3
Preparing Fiber

There are so many fun options for preparing your fiber for spinning. If you want to spin worsted yarns, look at the combs and hackles shown in this chapter. For woolen yarns, carders are the perfect tools to use. But don't be afraid to experiment with different types of fibers and tools and see what pretty blends of colors and textures you come up with for your yarns! All of these tools are fun to play with and would make a great addition to your fiber studio.

Opposite, clockwise from top left: Carded dyed fibers from hand cards or a drum carder; alpaca is one of the most popular fibers for spinners, because it is next-to-skin soft; you can easily blend and mix dyed wools without using any fiber processing equipment—simply hand-pick and tease out the locks with your fingers!
Top: Carded art batt by Esther Rogers
Bottom: Pulled roving by Elizabeth Stottlemeyer

Troubleshooting Tips

Problem: I want to blend many fibers together like a batt, but I don't own a drum carder.
Solution: Try using hand combs, hand carders, dog combs, or even your hands to blend the fiber together.

Problem: My fiber has a lot of vegetable matter in it. How can I remove it so my equipment doesn't get dirty?
Solution: Always skirt your fiber before washing, to remove as much vegetable matter as possible. Wash your fiber before using it on any equipment, to remove the grease and dirt. You can take small sections of fiber and shake it to loosen the vegetable matter before putting it through combs or hand carders. A wool picker is one of the best ways to get rid of vegetable matter. You may not be able to get rid of it, but when you spin the yarn it will continue to fall out. If you are finding there is so much vegetable matter in the fleece that after processing the fiber it still cannot be spun into yarn you can either send it to a mill to be professionally processed, or throw it away.

Problem: I want to purchase a drum carder, but I don't know which one to choose.
Solution: Drum carders come in wide and narrow sizes. The wider the drum carder, the more fiber you'll be able to include in your batts. Drum carders also come with fine and coarse teeth. Fine carders have more metal teeth per square inch. They are used for processing fine and luxury fibers such as angora, silk, and the finest wools. Fine carders also create a more blended batt. Coarse carders are best used for art batts, as they allow more of the fiber's natural texture (crimp or curl) to remain. They can also be used with luxury fibers, but take care that you don't rip or damage the finer fibers when using a coarse carder.

Equipment

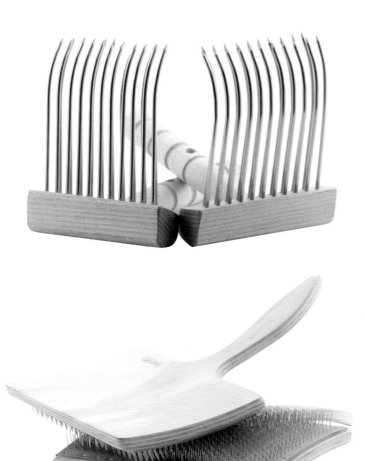

Here is a brief overview of the most common fiber processing tools and what they are used for. You can find free video tutorials on how to use all of these tools on www.youtube.com.

Always process clean, dry fiber on these tools. All of these tools can get vegetable matter out of fleeces, but it's always good to heavily skirt your fleece (see page 25) before washing and processing, to remove as much vegetable matter as possible and keep your processing tools clean.

Wool combs are for getting rid of guard hair, neps and noils (little bumps and pieces of fuzz), second cuts, and vegetable matter. After your fiber has been combed, you can pull the fiber from your combs as wool top and spin it into a worsted yarn.

Hand cards are for blending small amounts of fiber for woolen spinning. Once you have carded your fibers on hand cards, you can roll it into a rolag and spin it immediately. Hand cards also get rid of second cuts and vegetable matter.

Hackles are used for blending fiber and dizzing into roving for spinning. You can get a blending hackle for finer, more consistent fibers, or an art roving hackle for making chunky mixed-fiber rovings. You will need a diz to pull the fiber off your hackle. If your fiber has vegetable matter, some of it will fall out when using a hackle—but not all of it.

Top: Wool combs
Bottom: Hand cards

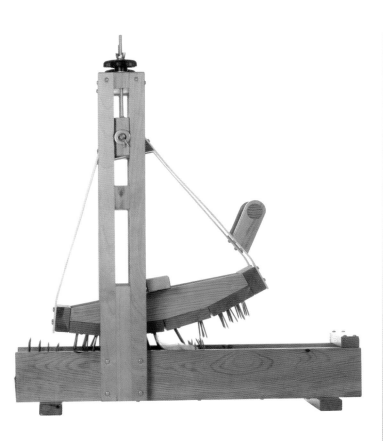

Wool pickers are used for fluffing and separating wool locks. You can also use your hands to pick wool locks, but if you want to process a whole fleece quickly from tight locks into clouds, a wool picker is the perfect tool for you. Wool pickers work best with long, medium, and coarse wools. Fine fibers will be damaged if put through a wool picker. The fiber you get from a wool picker is called picked wool. Wool pickers are great at getting a lot of vegetable matter out of fleeces.

Drum carders are among the most popular fiber processing tools on the market. There are fine carders for fibers such as angora and alpaca, or you can get a coarse carder for longwools and art batts. Drum carders are similar to hand cards, but they can process a lot more fiber in a shorter amount of time. The fiber you take off a drum carder is called a batt.

Top: Wool picker
Bottom: Drum carder

Processing Methods

The method of processing fiber determines what it is called. Following is a basic introduction to the different ways of preparing fiber and what kind of fiber they produce.

Roving

Roving has been carded—this means that the individual fibers are at random angles to each other. Roving is used to spin woolen yarns. Roving may look like top at first glance, but it spins a different yarn because of the random alignment of the fibers. You can make roving with an art hackle and a diz (see pages 50–51).

Batts

Batts have also been carded on a machine called a drum carder (see pages 44–45). Many artisans enjoy making "art batts" from random mixtures of plant and animal fibers and sparkle. Batts are also used for woolen yarns, and are a very popular way to spin art yarn. You can spin batts by stripping them apart, tearing off a chunk, or pulling them into strips of roving.

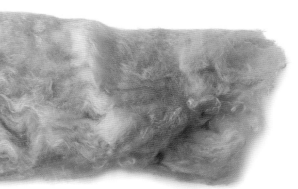

Top

Top has been combed—this means that the individual fibers are parallel to each other. You can create top by using hand combs, or you can buy commercially processed wool top from a mill. Top is used to spin worsted yarns.

Top: Blended roving
Middle: Carded batt of fiber
Bottom: Immersion-dyed wool top

Drafting Worsted vs. Woolen

There are two types of drafting that work well for beginners. Drafting is the process of pulling fibers from the bundle, and thinning them to the size yarn you want to spin. The more fibers that remain in the drafted area, the thicker your yarn will be; the fewer that remain in the drafted area, the finer your yarn will be. Choose one hand to hold the fiber (this will be your back hand) and the other hand to draft the fiber (your front hand).

Woolen (Forward)

With your front hand, pull the fiber toward the wheel and give the fiber to the wheel while your back hand keeps the twist from traveling into the fiber.

Worsted (Backward)

With your back hand, pull the fiber away from the wheel, as your front hand keeps the twist from traveling between your hands into the drafting zone. Then slide your front hand back over the drafting zone to allow the twist to travel onto the fiber, and give the length of yarn to the wheel.

Top: Single-ply wool/silk blend yarn spun using the worsted technique
Bottom: Two-ply yarn spun from wool roving using the woolen technique

Woolen characteristics	Worsted characteristics
Spun from short wool fibers (< 3 inches/7.5 cm)	Spun from longwool fibers (< 3 inches/7.5 cm)
Spun from medium or coarse wool fibers	Spun from fine wool fibers
Spun from roving or batts	Spun from top
Lower tensile strength	Higher tensile strength
Low to medium twist	Tight twist
Bulky, uneven yarn	Fine, smooth yarn
Fuzzy appearance	Smooth appearance
Heavier weight	Lighter weight
Less durable	More durable

Hand Picking Wool

To prepare wool locks for spinning into yarn, or for processing on the tool of your choice, you can use your bare hands. Always wash and thoroughly dry your fiber before hand picking.

1 Take a small handful of locks and pinch the ends with your fingers, while pulling your hands apart. If the locks are very thick, you can take individual locks and pull them apart to fluff them up and allow any vegetable matter to fall out of the lock.

2 The more you hand pick your wool locks, the less of the texture of the lock you will get in your finished product. You may decide to leave some curly texture and tips in your hand-picked locks when spinning.

Materials
Locks of wool

Using a Picker

You can make clouds of mixed fiber with a wool picker, or use the picker to remove vegetable matter from a washed fleece.

1 Make sure your wool is clean and dry before you put it through a picker, or the wool may be damaged. To use a wool picker, place a handful of wool locks in the front end of the picker, then swing the arm of the picker from back to front and back again.

2 The teeth on the picker swing will grab small amounts of wool locks and drag them through the teeth on the underside of the picker. As the locks are dragged through the nails, they are opened and separated into clouds.

3 Have a basket on the floor under the back end of the wool picker to catch the wool locks as they fall.

Materials
Wool picker | Locks of wool

+

It is good practice to wear leather gloves when using a wool picker, and to tie back long hair.

Some people find that fine fibers, such as angora or alpaca, become matted and ripped by the nails in a wool picker, but this is not always the case.

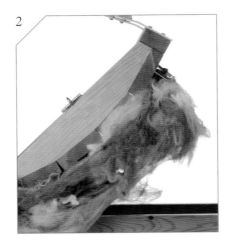

Combing Wool

Wool combs are used to remove shorter lengths of fiber (neps) and vegetable matter, as well as to align all the fibers in one direction. Combed fiber is called "top" and can be spun into worsted yarns.

1 With the tines pointing upward, take one of your wool combs and slide locks of fiber down the tines. Continue sliding locks down the tines until the comb is about half full.

2 (a) Hold the comb of fiber in front of you, then take the empty comb and slide it across and through the fiber with the tines facing away from you. As you continue combing in this direction, the fiber will transfer from one comb to the other.

(b) When no more fiber will transfer over, set it aside. Those are the shorter lengths (neps) of fiber. You can save them to use on a drum carder or art batts, but removing them will prevent pilling and fuzzing of your worsted spun yarns.

Materials
Wool combs | Locks of wool

1

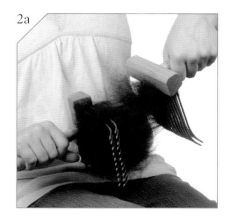

2a

2b

+ You can comb top traditionally using one type of wool, or mix several wools together to create your own unique blend.

3 To comb the fiber again, hold the full comb in your hand as before and, with the empty comb, run the tines through the fiber facing away from you. This will transfer the fiber to the empty comb, and remove more short fibers and neps from the wool.

4 Continue combing until no more neps or shorter lengths of fiber are left on the comb. Then gently, starting on one side of the comb, begin pulling the fiber off the comb into top. Roll the top into a ball, and it's ready for spinning. Compare the multicolored wools before combing (below), with the top from combed fleece (below right).

3

4

Using Hand Carders

Hand carding is a traditional method of preparing wool for spinning. The purpose of carding is to separate and straighten the wool fibers. Once your fibers have been carded, you can remove them from the hand carders as a batt or rolag of fluffy wool that is ready to spin.

1 To begin carding, lay the wool across the teeth of one hand carder. Continue adding the wool evenly across the entire card until the teeth are barely showing through.

2 Now take the second hand carder and place it over the first carder. Gently brush the top carder across the teeth of the bottom carder in a rolling motion. You will see the fibers transferring from the bottom hand carder to the top one. Continue brushing the fibers together until the fiber is evenly distributed on both carders.

Hand carders are wooden paddles with tiny wire teeth. You can find either coarse or fine wool carders. Coarse hand carders are best for carding wool and mohair. Fine carders are best for cotton and angora.

Materials
Clean animal fibers | Dyed animal fibers | Pair of hand carders

1

2

3 Continue carding, brushing the wool fiber from the bottom hand carder to the top, and as the top hand carder fills with wool, move it to become the bottom one.

4 When the fiber is well separated and fluffy, roll the fiber toward the handle of the carder to form a rolag that is ready for spinning. The brown rolag (below right) is made from one type of wool; the multicolored example (below) is made from different dyed wools.

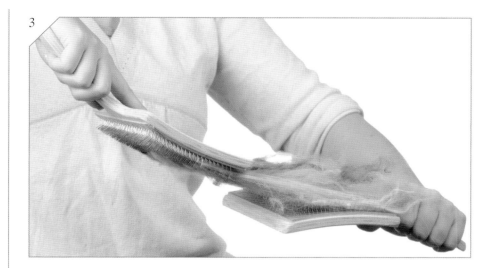

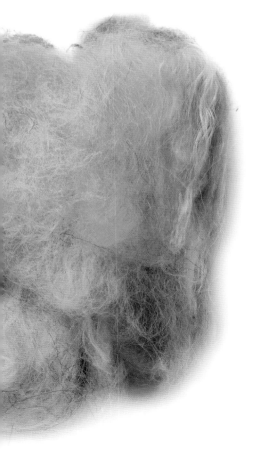

Blending on a Drum Carder

For beginners trying to blend fibers evenly on a drum carder, it is best to start with commercially processed fibers. For this tutorial you will be blending wool top with silk into a batt that would be perfect for spinning into sock yarn.

1 First start by pulling the wool top into even chunks to open the fibers and allow for better color blending. Take one of the chunks of wool and hold it on top of the drum carder. Turn the handle of the drum carder clockwise, and the teeth of the carder will gently grab the wool and pull it onto the drum. Continue adding chunks of wool across the entire carder, gently and evenly creating a uniform layer.

2 Now take the silk that you would like to add to the carder, and break it into small sections, about the size of your hand. Hold the silk over the drum of the carder and gently turn the handle. Allow the teeth of the carder to pull the silk onto the drum evenly. Continue adding silk evenly all the way across the drum carder, then add another layer of wool in the same way.

+

For even more blending, you can tear this batt into strips and put it through your carder again. Keep in mind that every time you put the dyed fibers through the carder, the colors will get more uniform. If you want more color variation, only card once. But for a completely even color tone, card two or more times until you've achieved the blend you are looking for.

Materials
Drum carder | Clean animal, plant, or synthetic fibers | Dyed animal, plant, or synthetic fibers | Doffer tool to release fiber

1

2

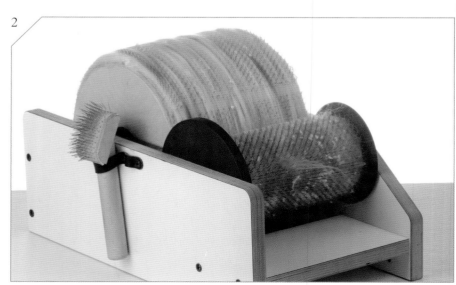

3 **(a and b)** Now find the break in the carder and use your doffer tool to gently pull the fibers off the carder. Roll the fibers into a batt for spinning.

3a

3b

Carding Art Batts on a Drum Carder

Art batts are fun for spinning into thick and thin, corespun, and other woolen yarns. You can put any fiber you can imagine into an art batt. For example, you could use blends of alpaca, wool, silk, bamboo, mohair, cotton, Firestar nylon, and Angelina sparkle.

1 Begin by carding a layer of wool or alpaca across the drum of the carder. Then begin "painting" fibers on top of the drum of the carder by holding them gently over the teeth while turning the drum carder handle.

2 Continue adding fibers at random throughout the batt. You can paint fiber stripes or sections of sparkle onto the batt to look like a landscape, or even close your eyes and grab a handful of fibers to add into the batt.

Materials
Drum carder | Clean animal, plant, or synthetic fibers | Dyed animal, plant, or synthetic fibers | Optional: scraps of fabric, ribbon, or novelty fibers | Doffer tool

+

Try mixing all your fibers for carding together in a bin. Then close your eyes and grab two handfuls of fiber. Card these fibers together into freeform art batts. This will help you create batts outside your color comfort zone.

3 On coarse carders, you can add curly wool locks to the final layer of the art batt to add amazing texture.

4 Once your carder is full, find the break in the carder and use your doffer tool to gently pull the fibers off the carder.

5 Roll the fibers into a batt for spinning.

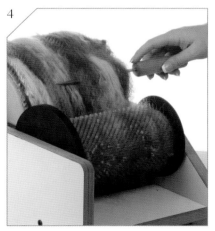

Building a Hackle

You can play with the dimensions of this art hackle to customize it for your fiber studio. A piece of wood from the craft store was used in this example, but any piece of wood that is at least 1 inch (2.5 cm) thick and 4 inches (10 cm) wide will work for an art hackle—it just needs to be long enough to attach combs. You can make your hackle as long as you want; the longer the hackle, the more roving you can diz off it. Also, you can use any strong plastic combs that have wide-set teeth.

1 Lay out your wood, combs, and screws to make sure you have the correct width and length for your wood.

2 Take the wooden piece and screw the combs into it securely.

3 Once all your combs have been screwed into the wood, attach the art hackle to the table with the table clamps. Now you can begin dizzing roving off your hackle (see pages 50–51).

Materials

Piece of wood (dimensions can vary based on what you have on hand, but make sure it is thick enough to attach the combs securely) | 3 plastic combs | 9 screws (3 per comb) | 2 table clamps to attach your art hackle to your table (not shown)

1
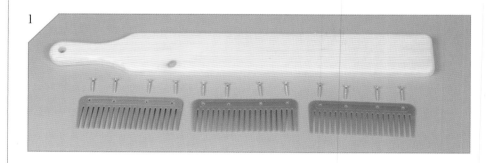

2

3

+
This hackle is safe to use with all fiber types, even including fine fibers such as angora and alpaca.

Dizzed fibre and hackle

Dizzing from a Hackle

How you layer your fiber will determine the look of the roving. Several layers of colors and fibers will give you a roving that will spin into a barber pole-type yarn. Layering single colors in vertical sections on your hackle will produce a self-striping or gradient roving.

1 To add wool fleece, take a handful and catch about 1 inch (2.5 cm) of the ends onto the top of the tines. Gently pull the fiber down onto the tines and back toward you, repeating down the hackle. To add mill top, slide one end onto the hackle and pull toward you, repeating down the hackle.

2 Make dizzing easier by gently tugging each layer to loosen it up. For whole locks, simply slide them onto the tines individually. You may layer fibers of various staple lengths and diz them off together successfully.

+ Use a diz with a ¼ inch (6 mm) opening for smooth roving, a ³⁄₁₆ inch (5 mm) opening for semi-smooth roving, and ³⁄₈ inch (10 mm) opening for textured and chunky roving.

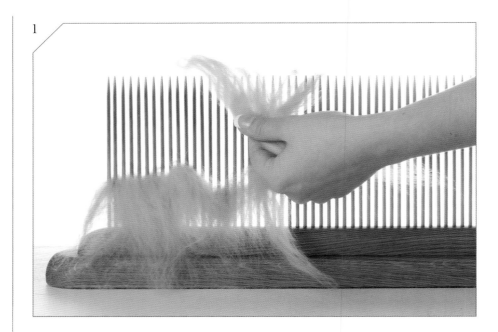

1

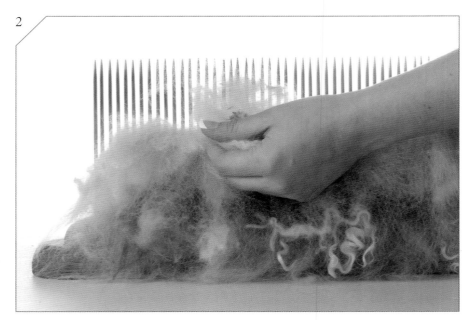

2

3 Once the hackle is full, fluff up your fibers to within the top ½ inch (1.25 cm) of the tines. Check the back of the hackle to see that the fiber is evenly distributed. Sometimes the front will look even but in the back there may still be compacted areas.

4 Gather up the ends of your fiber on one side, and twist the tip so it will fit through the hole in your diz. Holding the diz in one hand and the end of the fiber in the other, push the diz toward the hackle, then pull the fiber toward you and repeat. The distance of the pushing and pulling motion should not exceed the length of the shortest-stapled fiber in the roving. Continue in this way to create a length of roving. When you have dizzed all the fiber off the hackle, gently roll the roving into a ball.

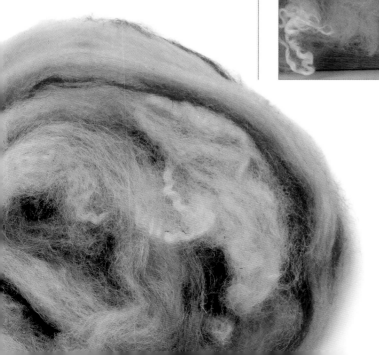

Gallery
Batts and Dizzed Fibers

Opposite: Blended batt by Lisa Renee McKenzie of Oscar & Sophia
Top: Blended batt carded by Kimberly Buchy
Bottom left: Dizzed and braided roving by Allison Findlay
Bottom right: Carded batt by Amber Churchill of Designs by Amber

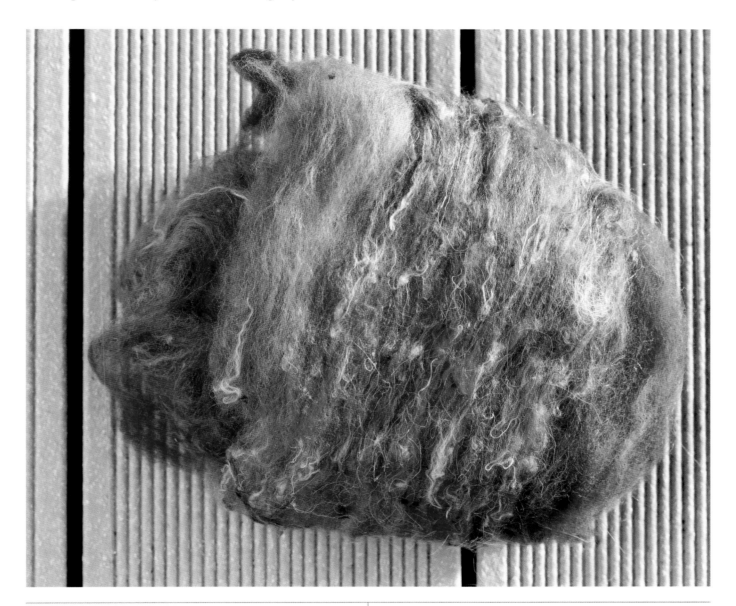

Opposite: Dizzed and braided roving
by Elizabeth Stottlemeyer of Hobbledehoy Fibers
Below: Carded art batt by Ashley Martineau of Neauveau Fiber Arts

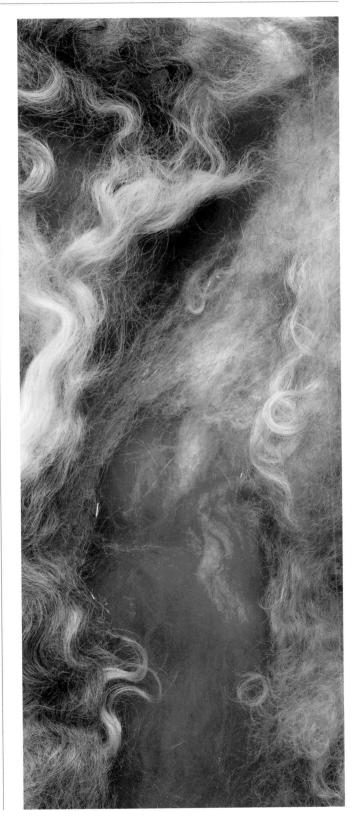

Below: Art batt by Esther Rogers of Jazz Turtle Creations
Opposite: Art batts carded by Sayra Adams of Atomic Blue Fiber

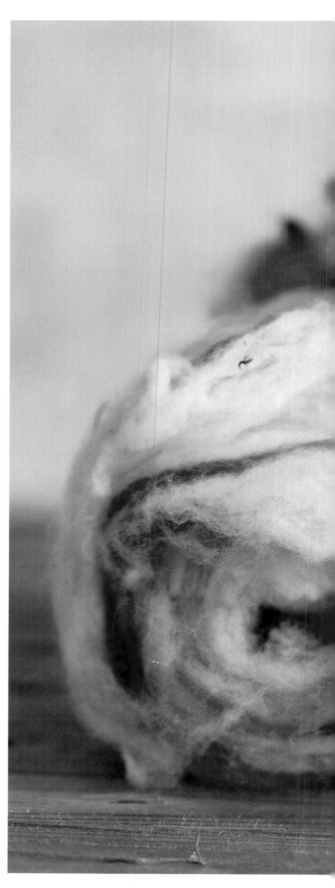

Tina Watson

Tina Watson of Herman Hills Farm in Ohio has been raising and breeding livestock for over 30 years. She is also a spinner and raises Wensleydale and Cormo sheep. When she hosts spin-ins on her farm, the spinners enjoy visiting the sheep and seeing some of the daily work involved in breeding and keeping wool sheep at first-hand.

Tina says: "Keeping livestock is a 24/7 365-days-a-year job. You cannot call in sick or take a spontaneous vacation. I tend to my sheep twice daily and watch them in the pastures in between that time. We grow our own hay in the summer, breed the ewes in the fall, and birth lambs in the spring—which is full of surprises, and sometimes heartaches."

When buying fleece direct from a shepherd, you will have the opportunity to learn about the animals who grew your fleece. Though it is easier to buy a fleece in person, many spinners don't have the option to go to a nearby farm or fiber festival. If you are buying online and are not familiar with the farm you are dealing with, you can always ask them to send you a sample of the fleece. Many shepherds will mail small samples for a minimal price.

"Most shepherds are in the business because they love the animals."

"Most shepherds are in the business because they love the animals. Fleece sales alone rarely cover all of the expenses involved in keeping fiber animals. When you buy a fleece directly from a farm, whether it is in person, online, or at a fiber festival, the money you spend helps the farmer cover farm expenses such as shearing and processing fibers, coats for the animals (in some cases), feed, hay, supplements, veterinary costs, and barn maintenance, as well as general farm/fencing maintenance."

"Personally, I believe nothing compares to starting with a raw fleece and ending with a beautiful handspun creation."

Fleeces take time and care to grow. Some shepherds spend time coating their flock to ensure a pristine fleece. All shepherds try to keep their pastures clear of burrs and other weeds, which can stick to the fleece. The fleeces on most fiber animals take a full year to grow. A lot can happen in a year in the life of an animal. By the time a spinner gets a shorn fleece the amount of time and effort it took to produce and protect that fleece cannot be measured.

Tina concludes: "Personally, I believe nothing compares to starting with a raw fleece and ending with a beautiful handspun creation."

Opposite, far left: Clean Cormo locks
Opposite: Clean naturally gray Wensleydale fleece
Above: Clean Wensleydale fleece

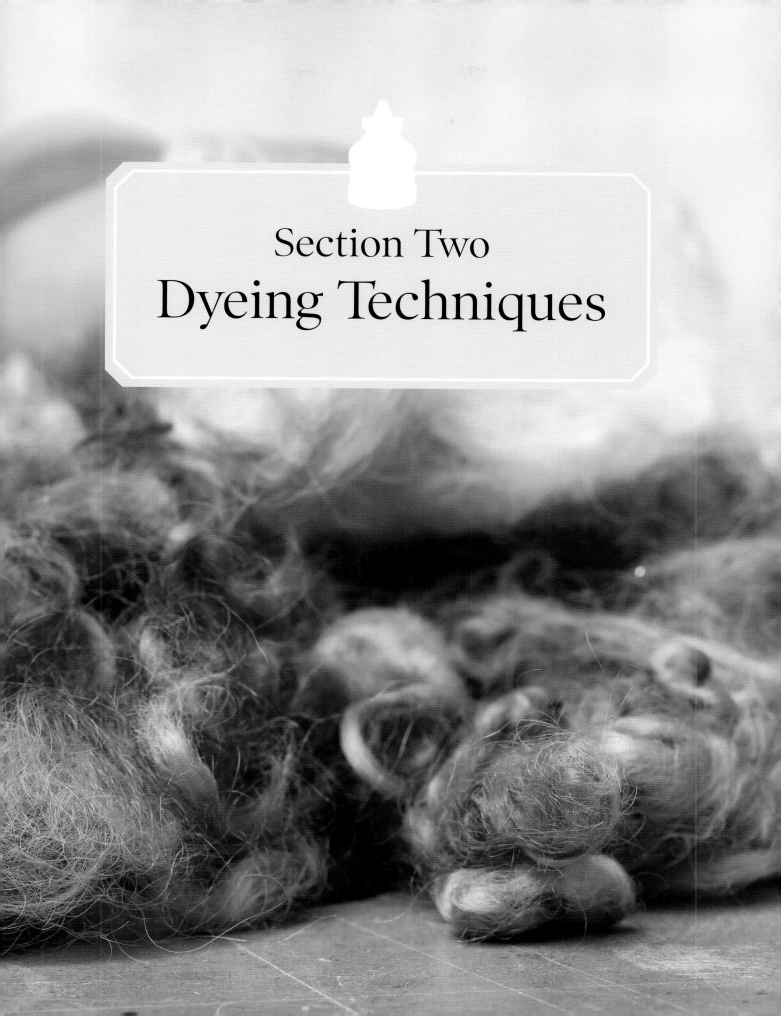

Section Two
Dyeing Techniques

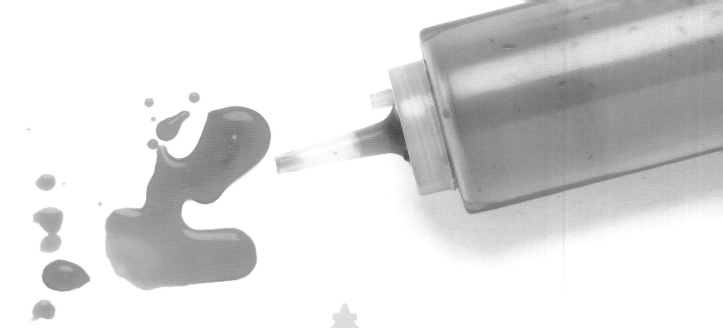

Chapter 4

Dyeing Fiber

All of the dyeing techniques in this book can be used for fiber before or after it is spun. Immersion dyeing gives you beautifully random dye lots of color. Gradient dyeing is perfect for projects you want to fade gracefully from dark to light. Hand painting creates a stunning striped effect. Tie dyeing is a method that is shown here using cotton, but that can be used on any plant fiber. Try dyeing fibers before spinning and after spinning to see the difference this makes to your finished knit or crochet projects. If you don't like the color of a dye lot you've made, simply over-dye it by following the instructions once more.

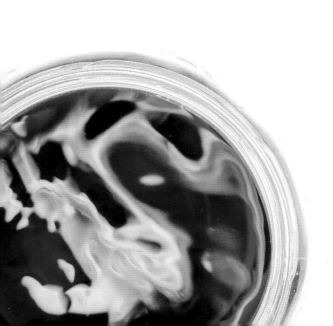

Troubleshooting Tips

Problem: When I am immersion dyeing, the water isn't turning clear.

Solution: Try adding more acid (white vinegar or citric acid work well) to the dyepot and allow the fiber to simmer for 15 more minutes. If the water still hasn't turned clear, it is possible that you used too much dye in the water and the fiber is already saturated with dye. You can add more fiber to the dyepot to soak up the remaining dye, or add less dye to the next dyepot.

Problem: When I am solar dyeing, the water isn't turning clear.

Solution: It is possible that your jars aren't getting hot enough. Try wrapping the jars in a black plastic bag the following hot day to complete the dyeing process. Or place your jars of fiber in a dyepot of water (similar to canning fruit) without lids and simmer for 30 minutes. Make sure the water in the dyepot does not flow into the open jars of fiber (so the dyes do not mix). After the water has turned clear, allow the dyepot to cool, then remove the jars.

Problem: When I am hand painting or gradient dyeing, my colors run together.

Solution: Try rolling your fiber in a different direction in the plastic. Roll it from end to end instead of lengthwise. Also try adding more citric acid in the dyeing process so that the fiber absorbs the dye more quickly.

Opposite, clockwise from top: Try using condiment bottles (found online, or in the kitchen accessories section of your local store) to squirt the dye onto your fiber; dye powders can be toxic, so read the label and wear gloves and a mask if your dye contains heavy metals—you can also work with nontoxic dyes, such as food dyes or specialist nontoxic brands; follow the directions on commercial dyes to determine the correct powder-to-water ratio

Top: Dyed silk by Mary Egbert
Bottom: Dyed wool locks by Ashley Martineau

Animal Fiber

Animal fibers such as wool, angora, alpaca, mohair, and silk are easy to dye using a method called acid dyeing. The "acid" refers to the pH of the water—acidic water causes the dye to adhere permanently to the fiber. Water can be turned acidic by the addition of vinegar, citric acid, or even lemon juice.

Acid dyes are sold in powdered form and are dissolved in water. However, you can also use food coloring, Easter egg dyes, frosting paste dyes, and Kool-aid packets (unsweetened packets) instead of commercial acid dyes. Darker colors can be achieved by adding more dye, and lighter colors by adding less dye.

In order to adhere the dye permanently to the fiber, heat must be applied. Many dyers use a microwave as their heat source, some use a crockpot, and others use the stovetop. In the summer you can dye wool on a camping stove, or using solar power (in the sun).

If the correct amount of dye has been used, the water will be almost clear or milky white when the dye has exhausted into the fiber. This is because the wool has absorbed all of the dye particles. If you add too much dye, your water will never turn clear. For this reason, be conservative with the amount of dye you use—a little goes a long way.

Left: Dyed wool top by Patricia Briceño

Above: Dyed silk cocoons by Camaj.
These cocoons have been dyed after
the silkworm has been removed

Plant Fiber

Plant fibers (cotton, linen, rayon, hemp, ramie, and bamboo) are dyed using a method called fiber-reactive dyeing. Fiber-reactive dyes are also known as cold-water dyes because they do not require heat to make them permanent.

Fiber-reactive dyes require an alkaline environment to permanently adhere to the fiber. A common base for dyeing plant fiber is soda ash (sodium carbonate). It's best to buy soda ash in its pure form from a dye supplier. Because soda ash is caustic and these dyes will temporarily stain your skin, wear disposable latex or vinyl gloves while you work.

Different plant fibers will take different amounts of dye. For example, linen will dye a slightly different color than cotton—even if they are the same color naturally. Rayon absorbs dye vigorously and becomes saturated with any color. The end result also depends on the color of the original fiber. A natural ivory or honey-colored fiber will end up duller in color than a bright white fiber.

Left: Dyed bamboo fiber

Synthetic Fiber

Synthetic fiber (nylon) can be dyed using the same instructions as all of the wool dyeing tutorials in this book. (See pages 68–77.)

Here are some types of nylon that will take dye just like wool:

- faux cashmere
- faux angora
- faux mohair
- Snow mountain nylon
- Firestar nylon
- wool/nylon blends

To dye synthetic fibers, simply use an acid dye and either citric acid or vinegar to set the dye to the fiber. Bear in mind that nylon can melt, so keep your dye pot on a low simmer. Never boil or leave your dye pots unattended.

Above: Immersion-dyed Firestar (nylon) fiber by Samantha LaRue

Immersion Dyeing

Immersion dyeing is a fun way to dye synthetic fiber, wool top, and locks—and it always produces unique results. If you like getting a different result every time you dye, you'll love immersion dyeing.

1 First, fill the pot half-full of water. Add 1 cup (240 ml) of vinegar or 2 tbsp (30 ml) citric acid, whichever you prefer.

2 Add your wool or synthetic fiber to the pot. Press the fiber down into the water until it's saturated. Heat the water on the stovetop; you want it steaming hot, but not boiling. After raising the temperature of the water, sprinkle or pour on your dye.

Want to duplicate a dyelot? Immersion dyeing creates random effects, but if you keep track of the colors and amounts of dye you used you can create a similar dyelot.

You can use many different dyes for this tutorial. Gel frosting dyes, food coloring, commercial powder dyes, and even Easter egg dyes work well. Mix and match different types of dyes for truly unique results.

Materials

Large stainless-steel pot | Water | Acid (vinegar or citric acid) | Wool (top or locks) or synthetic (nylon) fiber | Acid dye | Potato masher

3 After letting the wool sit in the hot water (be careful that it doesn't boil) for 20 minutes, press the wool down into the pot with the potato masher to see if the water has turned clear. If the water still has dye in it, add a dash of vinegar or citric acid and allow the wool to sit for another 10 minutes on the stove.

Once the water has turned clear, all of the dye has been absorbed. Allow the pot of wool to cool, then gently remove the wool from the pot, rinse it, and place it on your drying rack. Compare the dyed longwool locks with the dyed wool top (bottom left and right).

3

Gradient Dyeing

Gradient dyeing is simply producing a color effect that goes from dark to light. The principle is simple—it's all about mixing shades of dye. Be creative, and experiment with different shades, different colors, and different gradients.

1 First, fill a bowl half-full of cool water. Add ¼ cup (60 ml) vinegar or 2 tbsp (30 ml) citric acid. Add the wool top to the bowl and let it soak for 15 minutes. (You can reuse this solution later.) Remove excess water by squeezing the wool gently, wearing rubber gloves.

2 Half fill the jar with water and mix in 1 tbsp (15 ml) dye. This will be your darkest shade, and you will use it to mix the rest of your dyes. Stir until all of the dye has dissolved in the water.

3 (a) Fill each of the plastic bottles half full of water. In the first bottle, mix 10 tbsp (150 ml) dye from the jar.

(b) In the second bottle, mix 6 tbsp (90 ml) dye from the jar.

(c) In the third bottle, mix 4 tbsp (60 ml) dye from the jar. To darken the entire gradient, add 1 tbsp (15 ml) dye from the jar to each bottle until you reach your preferred depth of color. To lighten the gradient, add the same amount of water to each jar.

Materials

Large bowl | Water | Acid (vinegar or citric acid) | Wool top | Rubber gloves | Acid dye | 1-quart (1-liter) glass jar | 3 plastic squirt bottles | Plastic wrap | Microwave-safe glass bowl

1

2

3a

3b

3c

4 **(a)** Lay out a snake of wool on top of a sheet of plastic wrap and squirt the darkest value onto the first coil.

(b) Add the color from the first bottle to the second coil.

(c) Continue until you've used up all the shades.

5 **(a)** Roll the plastic wrap over each section of wool to form a barrier that will stop the dye leaking from one coil into the next. Carefully seal the plastic wrap ends to prevent leakage, and place in a microwave-safe glass bowl.

(b) Microwave on high for 5 minutes. Check to see whether the wool has absorbed the dye. If not, microwave on high for 3 minutes more. Let the wool cool, and rinse with lukewarm water to remove any excess dye.

4a
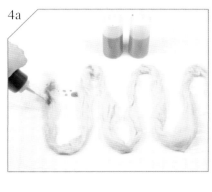

4b
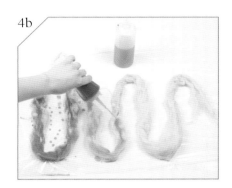

4c
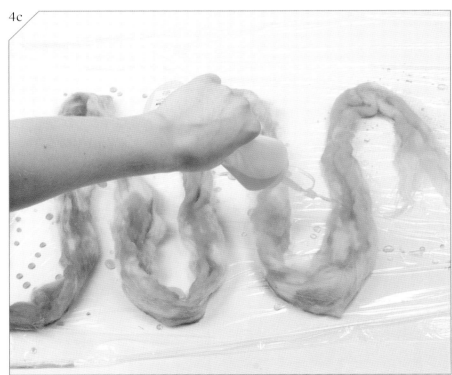

5a

5b
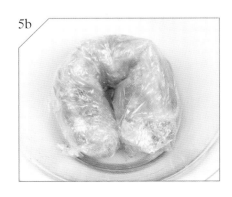

Hand Painting

The secret of hand painting is to not overlap your dye colors, but to use water to blend them together seamlessly. You'll find that using this technique lends itself to softer color transitions and more control over secondary colors.

1 First, fill a bowl half-full of cool water. Add ¼ cup (60 ml) vinegar or 2 tbsp (30 ml) citric acid. Add the wool top to the bowl and let it soak for 15 minutes. (You can reuse this solution later.) Remove excess water by squeezing the wool gently, wearing rubber gloves.

2 **(a)** Mix your dyes into three of the plastic squirt bottles. You can make them as light or as dark as you like. Make sure all of the dye has dissolved into the water. Cover your dyeing workspace with plastic wrap. Lay out a length of wool on top of the plastic wrap, and squirt on your first dye color.

(b) Leave a 3-inch (7.5-cm) space between the first color and the second color.

(c) Continue adding sections of each color to your wool top. You can dye long sections or short sections in an unlimited number of colors.

+ You can also hand paint individual longwool locks.

Materials

Large bowl | Water | Acid (vinegar or citric acid) | Wool top | Rubber gloves | 3 colors of acid dye | 4 plastic squirt bottles | Plastic wrap | Microwave-safe glass bowl

1
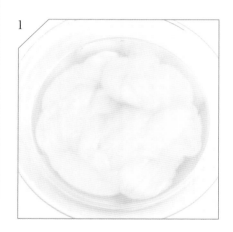

2a
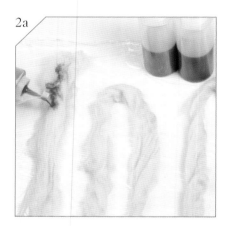

2b
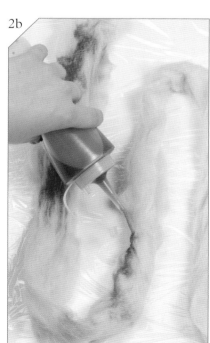

2c
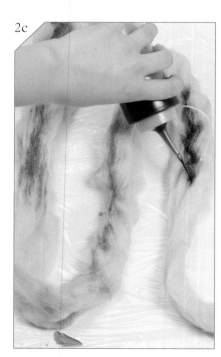

3 **(a)** Once you have dyed the lengths of fiber, go back between each color and use a squirt bottle filled with water to saturate the wool in between the colors.

(b and c) Then wrap the wool in plastic wrap and squish the saturated area to blend the colors together.

4 Carefully seal the plastic wrap ends to prevent leakage, and place in a microwave-safe glass bowl. Microwave on high for 5 minutes. Check to see whether the wool has absorbed the dye. If not, microwave on high for 3 minutes more. Let the wool cool, and rinse with lukewarm water to remove any excess dye.

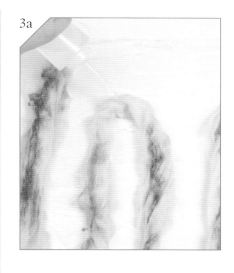

3a

3b

3c

4

Solar Dyeing

Solar dyeing is a great way to dye wool in hot climates in the summertime. Keep in mind that you will need several hours of hot direct sunlight for the dye to set—check the weather forecast before you begin.

Solid colors

1 Fill a large pot with water and a few tablespoons of citric acid and set on the stove to boil. Measure out the fiber in 2–4 oz (57–114 g) bundles, and place in a bowl of warm water to soak. Add dye to the jars. Keep in mind that some fibers require more dye than others, and measure accordingly.

2 Pour the boiling acidic water into the jars (use the measuring cup), and fill them ¾ full.

3 Add fiber from the bowl to each jar, pressing down with a skewer. If necessary, fill to the top of the jar with more acidic water.

4 Once you have prepared your jars, put lids on them and set them outside in direct sunlight. If they need extra heat, put the jars on top of a black plastic trash bag or, put them inside the bag and tie the top for maximum heat.

Materials

Large pot and slightly smaller pot | Water | Citric acid | Protein fiber | Bowl | Acid dyes | Large canning jars (1 per dye) | Measuring cup | Wooden skewers | Black trash bags (optional)

Multiple colors

1 Fill a large pot with water and set it on the stove to boil. Fill another slightly smaller pot with water and add 2 tbsp (30 ml) citric acid. Measure out the fiber in 2–4 oz (57–114 g) bundles, and place a dry bundle of fiber into each jar.

2 Add the dye on top of the dry fiber.

3 Then add the boiling water (use the measuring cup). As the hot water filters down the jar it will carry the dye down with it. This creates a beautiful tie-dye effect. Keep adding boiling water to the jar until it's ¾ full. Top off the jar with acidic water.

Once you have prepared your jars, put lids on them and set them outside in direct sunlight. If your jars need extra heat, put the jars on top of a black plastic trash bag. Or, put the jars inside the bag and tie the top for maximum heat.

For the dye to set, the temperature has to be at 185°F (85°C) for at least 30 minutes. Leaving the jars out in direct sunlight for 3–4 hours will achieve this. If your dyes are not setting, place the jars (without lids) in the microwave to raise the temperature and set the dye. When the dye is set the water will be clear.

Tie Dyeing

This method is for dyeing cotton and other plant fibers. This technique will not work on any animal (protein) fibers or synthetic fibers. You can use it for plant fibers in any form— try dyeing the fiber before you spin it, and dyeing the yarn after it's been spun to achieve different effects.

1 Take the plant fibers you want to dye and soak them in a glass bowl of water and soda ash. For a large bowl of water, a spoonful of soda ash will suffice. If you are dyeing larger portions, follow the measurements on your soda ash package.

2 While the fiber is soaking, prepare your dyeing area by covering it with plastic wrap. This will protect any surfaces from getting stained from the dye. Soak the fiber for about 10 minutes. Then squeeze the water out of the fiber and place it on the plastic wrap.

Materials

Cotton/Plant fiber to dye | Glass bowl | Water | Soda ash | Plastic wrap | Plant-specific dyes | Dye bottles | Urea | Plastic bag

3 Mix the dye in your dye bottles following the manufacturer's instructions. Also add a spoonful of urea to help the dye dissolve in the water. Make sure all the urea has dissolved before applying the dye to the fiber. Squirt the mixed dye onto the fiber. You can use as many colors as you like. Try out different techniques (see "Gradient Dyeing" on pages 70–71 and "Hand Painting" on pages 72–73) on cotton or flax top fiber.

4 Wrap the cotton in the plastic wrap, then place the wrapped cotton into a plastic bag and let it sit for at least 4 hours. For the best dye absorption, allow the fiber to set overnight.

After the dye has had time to set into the fiber, run the fiber under cold water and squeeze out the excess dye until the water runs clear. Lay the fiber out on your drying rack (see pages 28–29) and allow to fully dry before spinning, carding, or using on your fiber equipment.

For dyeing a plant fiber that has been processed into top—try squirting the dye on the fiber as you would using the gradient technique (see pages 70–71) or hand painting (see pages 72–73) to create a gradient or striped effect on the fiber.

3

4

Gallery

Dyed Fibers

Opposite: Silk lap dyed by Karla Muntane of Spinning Mermaid Fibers
Below: Dyed top by Kate Heffer of Knits and 'Nacks

Opposite: Merino top dyed by Marcella Hogg of Hogg Wild Fibers
Top: A collection of dyed wool blend tops by Sarah Hollandsworth of Yarn Geek Fibers
Above: Hand-dyed wool roving by Rachel Kluesner of Dyeabolical
Left: Dyed Merino top by Patti Richards of Funky Yarns

Lexi Boeger

Lexi Boeger is one of the modern pioneers of the free-spinning movement. Her yarns have inspired countless others to learn how to spin, or to look at yarn from a fresh perspective.

Lexi says: "Don't worry about what anybody else does, or what's come before you. Don't try to know it all before you start. Keep it simple, because it is simple. Make your experience about you and the fiber in your hand. Listen to your material and have the confidence to try your ideas when they come to you. There is no failure, only the gaining of knowledge.

"Listen to your material and have the confidence to try your ideas when they come to you."

"There is a real danger in trying to hold on too tightly to ownership of ideas. My philosophy? Listen for ideas, put them out there as best as you can, put your beautiful stamp on it … but don't try and keep it forever—let it go, move on to the next one."

Lexi is deeply inspired by the fiber itself. "I have to say that the fleece and material actually speak to me. My hands hear what it wants to be, so I just follow that voice. During the spinning process there is a two-way conversation between me and the fiber. The fiber chooses what it wants to do, and I let it while still making sure it is structurally sound."

Lexi is an award-winning artist, and her work hangs in galleries around the world. She has published three books (*Handspun Revolution*, *Intertwined*, and *Handspun*) and also designed and produced the AURA spinning wheel with Majacraft. With help from the worldwide spinning community, Lexi created the Giant Skein—the longest skein of handspun yarn in the world. She launched Yarnival—the world's first fiber festival devoted to the genre of free spinning—after having built the community-based Pluckyfluff Studio with funds donated from spinners around the world. She teaches spinning workshops worldwide (you can see her schedule at www.pluckyfluff.com).

Lexi's goal is to grow Yarnival (www.yarnival.org) into the most renowned free-spinning event in the world, with an annual publication to showcase new and upcoming spinners, fiber producers, and designers from around the world. "I want to devote my energies to growing this craft and providing help and support for others in the field. Other than that I want to always enjoy making. I want my kids to stay happy and healthy and I hope to provide them with the same encouraging freedom I was given so that they will be able to pursue their own visions."

"The fiber chooses what it wants to do, and I let it while still making sure it is structurally sound."

Opposite: These yarns were both first corespun (see page 102) from a carded art batt (see page 46), then plied using the coil technique (see page 145), then Navajo plied (see page 149). Lexi calls this combination of techniques a "Coil Boil," and it is one of her signature yarns
Top left: Detail of pink Coil Boil (shown left), by Lexi Boeger
Top right: Norway Art Yarn by Lexi Boeger

Section Three
Spinning Techniques

Chapter 5

Drop Spindles

The drop spindle is one of the oldest known spinning tools in history. It is portable, and is often used to create finely spun, traditional yarns. This chapter covers three basic spinning techniques on a drop spindle, as well as instructions for building your own spindle.

Opposite, clockwise from top left: Yarn by Allison Jai; dyed wool locks by Robyn Story; drop spindle full of yarn by Ashley Martineau
Top: Yarn by Brittany Wilson
Bottom: Handknit cowl by Michelle Snowdon

Troubleshooting Tips

Problem: The twist travels up into all my fiber and makes it impossible to draft.
Solution: Hold a smaller amount of fiber in your hand (if you are spinning from a batt or locks) or predraft your fiber (if you are spinning roving or top). Pinch the fiber with your fingers to prevent the twist from traveling up into the fiber in your hand.

Problem: My spindle starts spinning in the opposite direction while I'm drafting, untwisting the fiber.
Solution: Spin the spindle, and park it between your knees while sitting down. Then draft your fiber so the twist travels up into the fiber. Continue spinning (building up twist), parking the spindle (to keep it from spinning in the opposite direction), and drafting the twist up into the fiber.

Problem: My fiber is overtwisted.
Solution: Draft more fiber before spinning the spindle again, or allow the spindle to spin in the opposite direction before winding your yarn.

Problem: I want to create an even, traditional yarn and I keep getting thick and thin sections.
Solution: It takes practice to create a perfectly even, traditional yarn. But you can make it easier by predrafting your fiber before spinning.

Problem: I want to create a thicker yarn, but the spindle simply won't keep spinning.
Solution: Your spindle is too light for the thickness of yarn you want to spin. Try using a heavier-weight spindle.

Problem: My yarn falls apart after it's been spun.
Solution: You aren't putting enough twist into the fiber when you're spinning. Make sure you can see the twist going up the fiber, creating a round cylindrical yarn, and holding on to the twisted yarn while you wrap it onto the staff of the spindle—not losing any of the twist you have created in the fiber.

Choosing a Drop Spindle

When choosing a drop spindle you need to consider whether you want a top whorl or a bottom whorl, and how bulky or fine you want to spin.

Top whorl means that the whorl (the wheel of the spindle) is near the top, closer to the hook. These spindles usually spin faster and are often lighter than bottom whorl spindles. If you want to spin finer yarns, top whorl would be the perfect place to start.

Bottom whorl spindles have the whorl near the bottom of the spindle, farther from the hook. Many spinners prefer bottom whorl spindles for plying because they spin longer than top whorl spindles. Bottom whorl spindles are often used to spin bulky yarns.

To spin a bulky yarn, you will need a heavier spindle. For a finer yarn, you will need a lighter spindle. Below is a spindle weight reference chart to help you choose the weight of spindle you will need.

Weight of yarn	Weight of spindle
Laceweight	½ oz (14 g)
Fingering	1 oz (28 g)
Sport/DK	1¾ oz (50 g)
Worsted weight	2½ oz (70 g)
Bulky	3 oz (85 g) plus

Still can't decide what kind of spindle to choose? Try making both top whorl and bottom whorl spindles (see pages 90–91) to determine which style and weight works best for you.

+ Drop spindling is a great way to teach young children how to spin yarn. Even 5-year-olds can learn how to spin yarn on a drop spindle.

Top: Lightweight top-whorl spindle for spinning laceweight yarns
Bottom: Bulky student top-whorl spindle for spinning medium-weight and bulky yarns
Opposite: Single yarn by Ashley Martineau of Neauveau Fiber Arts

Building a Drop Spindle

The wooden drop spindle will weigh about 2 oz (57 g) when complete. With it you will be ready to spin fine to worsted weight yarns. The upcycled drop spindle makes clever use of old household objects you may have lying around.

Wooden

1 Put a ring of glue around the dowel about 2 inches (5cm) from the end, and slide the wheel onto the dowel and over the glue.

2 Wait for the glue to dry before attaching the cup hook and starting to spin. Attach the hook to the end near the whorl for a top-whorl spindle and at the opposite end for a bottom-whorl spindle. Paint the spindle if you like. Let the paint dry thoroughly before starting to spin.

Materials

1 wooden wheel with a ⅜ inch (1 cm) hole | 1 × 12-inch (30-cm) wooden dowel, ⅜ in (1 cm) diameter | Wood glue | 1 × ½ inch (1.25 cm) cup hook | Paint (optional)

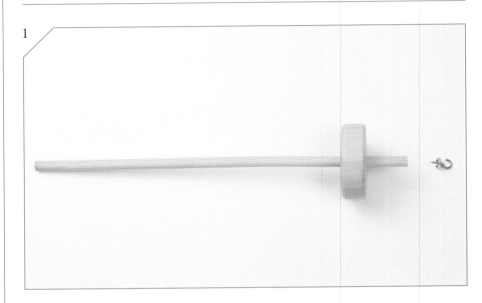

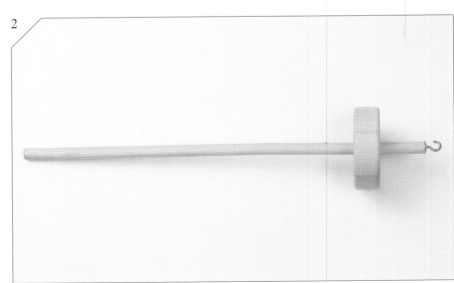

Upcycled

1 Take one of the rubber bands (or hair elastics) and wrap it around the dowel about 3 inches (7.5 cm) from the top of the dowel.

2 Slide the CDs onto the dowel and secure with the other rubber band. Roll the rubber bands (or hair elastics) snugly against the CDs to secure them.

3 Take one of the cup hooks and screw it into the dowel. The hook will be at the top for both a top whorl and a bottom whorl spindle. Decorate the spindle by drawing on it with a black permanent marker if you like.

+
To add more weight to the spindle and spin bulkier yarn, add more CDs between the rubber bands.

Materials

1 × ½ inch (1.25 cm) cup hook | 1 × 12 inch (30 cm) wooden dowel, ⅜ inch (1 cm) diameter | 2 old CDs | 2 rubber bands or hair elastics | Black permanent marker (optional)

1

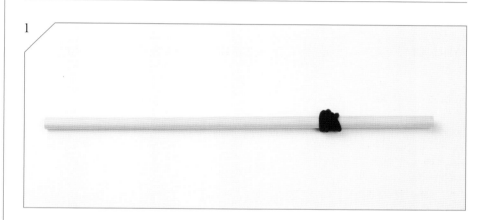

2

3

Spinning

Before you start, you will need to make a leader thread for the drop spindle. Take 24 inches (60 cm) of strong cotton thread and tie the ends in a knot. Slip knot that thread around the staff of the spindle three times, then wrap the thread around the spindle to secure it. Take the end loop of the leader thread and wrap it around the hook twice. This will be how you begin spinning any yarn on your drop spindle.

1 Loop the end of the fiber through the leader thread loop. Twist the spindle with your hands in a clockwise direction while holding onto the end of the fiber. You will feel the twist traveling up into the fiber. Slide your finger back and you will see the twist travel up into the fiber and start to turn the fiber into yarn.

2 Spin the drop spindle with your hand and slowly let it drop as the twist travels up the fiber. To load the yarn onto the spindle, hold the spindle so you don't lose any twist, unhook the yarn from the hook, and wrap it around the spindle under the whorl. Then loop the end of the yarn through the hook twice, and continue spinning.

+ Try using pencil roving if you are new to drop spindling—this is ready to spin without any drafting. Drop spindling requires multitasking, so the simpler you can make your first time spinning, the better—you will gain confidence as you learn.

Materials
Drop spindle | Fiber prepared for spinning (roving, top, or batt)

3 Once you are comfortable with spinning fiber and wrapping it around your spindle, you can practice spinning while drafting from wool top or an art batt. The less fiber you hold in your hand, the easier it will be to control. Loop the beginning of the fiber through the leader thread, and spin the spindle in a clockwise direction, letting the twist travel up into the fiber. Continue spinning the spindle in a clockwise direction, and gently pull the fiber out of your hand. If the spindle slows down, stop drafting and spin the spindle.

Drafting is when you are pulling the fiber from your hand. This allows the twist to travel up small portions of the fiber at a time. This gives you control over how thick the yarn becomes. The more fiber you draft, the thinner the yarn will be.

Corespinning

Corespinning is spinning fiber onto or around an existing yarn—the core yarn. Depending on how you spin, the core might be completely covered, or it might show. Many spinners prefer a core that is the same fiber as what they will be spinning around it. Experiment with different core threads to see what works for you.

1 Attach the core to the leader. Take a small amount of fiber and pinch it around the core thread while the spindle is spinning.

2 Continue spinning in a clockwise direction and allow the fiber to wrap around the core thread at a 90-degree angle.

3 When it becomes awkward to spin because of the length of yarn you have made, unhook the leader thread from the spindle hook and wrap the yarn around the spindle.

Materials
Drop spindle | Carded batt (see page 44 for a blended batt and page 46 for an art batt)

1

2

3

+ Take the core thread and loop it through the leader thread loop on your drop spindle. Then begin spinning the drop spindle clockwise so the twist travels up the loop and into the core thread, to secure it. That way, when you begin spinning the fiber, the spindle won't fall to the ground.

Plying

Plying can be done to make the yarn more durable, or to make it more interesting and decorative. You can change the look of the yarn by changing the angle at which you ply.

1 Take the plying thread and tie it into a knot with the handspun yarn. Take this knot and put it into the loop of the leader thread. Begin spinning the drop spindle counterclockwise so the twist travels up the loop and tightens around the knot of yarn. That way, when you begin plying the yarn the spindle won't fall to the ground.

2 Continue spinning in a counterclockwise direction while holding the plying thread and the yarn in a "V"-shape with your fingers. You can see how the twist travels up and wraps the two yarns together to make a 2-ply yarn. Once you have a long length of yarn, stop spinning and wrap the yarn around the drop spindle.

3 **(a)** To make a more textured ply, hold the handspun yarn at a 90-degree angle to the plying thread. It is very important to have a strong plying thread if you use this technique, because all the weight of the yarn relies on the strength of that thread.

(b) Play with different angles to achieve different effects when you're plying.

+

In general, you ply in the opposite direction from that in which the yarn was originally spun.

Materials

Drop spindle | Handspun single yarn (see page 92 on spinning a single) | Plying thread

1
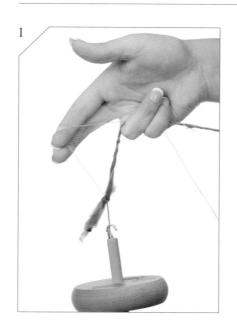

2

3a

3b

Chapter 6

Kick Spindles

A kick spindle is a larger version of a drop spindle that rests on the floor and allows you to use both hands to draft and spin yarn. A kick spindle is a great compromise between a wheel and a drop spindle. This tool can create traditional, finely spun yarns as well as large, bulky art yarns. You can find handcrafted kick spindles on www.etsy.com or build your own using the tutorial in this book.

Troubleshooting Tips

Problem: My kick spindle doesn't spin for a long period of time. How can I get it to spin for longer?
Solution: Try adding oil to the well where the spindle rests. This may be a ball bearing, or the thimble of your handcrafted spindle. This oil will create lubrication that will help your spindle spin for a longer period of time between each draft.

Problem: I'm finding it uncomfortable to use a kick spindle. What can I do to make it more comfortable?
Solution: Make sure the chair you are sitting in allows you to have good posture when spinning. This applies to spinning with a drop spindle and a wheel as well. Also, try chairs with different heights to see if you are more comfortable at a higher or lower angle than the kick spindle. You can also turn your spindle around and kick with the other foot to see if that is more comfortable for you.

Problem: My kick spindle slides across the floor when I'm using it. How can I prevent that?
Solution: Glue a piece of rubbery shelf liner to the base of the spindle to keep it from sliding across the floor.

Problem: Is there a way for me to use my kick spindle without using my feet?
Solution: Sure! Place it on a tabletop and use one of your hands to spin the whorl.

Opposite, clockwise from top left: Recycled yarn by Ashley Martineau; randomly plied yarn by Ashley Martineau; you can achieve a ply effect in a single by holding a thread alongside the fiber as you spin the single, as shown here
Top: Yarn by Nicole Constantin
Bottom: Yarn by Kristine Haddock

Building a Kick Spindle

A kick spindle may also be called a Mother Marion Wheel and is easy to make using readily available materials. A heavier base will keep your kick spindle from sliding across the floor when you are using it.

1 The base used here was a piece of 2-inch (5-cm) thick wood that measured 7 x 9 inches (18 x 23 cm). You can use any size of wooden base, as long as it's thick enough to drill into. Drill an indentation (with a drill fitted with a ½-inch/13-mm bit) at a 45-degree angle into the base of your wood. Place the thimble into this indentation. You can glue the thimble into the indentation if it is loose. When you are ready to spin, place some oil into the thimble to help the spindle spin freely without drag.

2 Take the support beam of your spindle (this one was 1-inch/2.5-cm square and 8 inches/20 cm high) and drill a ½-inch (13-mm) hole through the center of it at a 45-degree angle.

3 Attach the support beam to the base of the kick spindle with a screw.

Materials

2½-foot (75-cm) long ½-inch (13 mm) hardwood dowel | 1 large wooden bun foot | 1 small wooden bun foot | Wooden base | Wooden spindle support | Thimble | ½-inch (13-mm) brass hook | Screw | Oil (optional) | Drill and drill bit

1
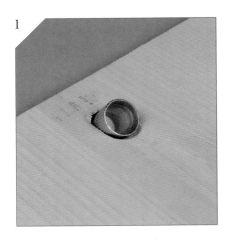

2

3

+

To keep your kick spindle from sliding across the floor, try gluing an antislip pad to the base to keep it stable while you're spinning.

4 Drill a ½-inch (13-mm) hole through the center of the large bun foot and small bun foot. Slide the dowel through the 45-degree hole into the support, and before you place the base of it into the thimble, slide it through the large bun foot. Place the bottom of the dowel into the thimble and adjust the bun foot so that it is between the thimble and the support.

5 Now slide the small bun foot onto the dowel so that it rests against the support beam.

6 Screw the ½-inch (13-mm) brass hook into the top of the spindle. The kick spindle is ready to use!

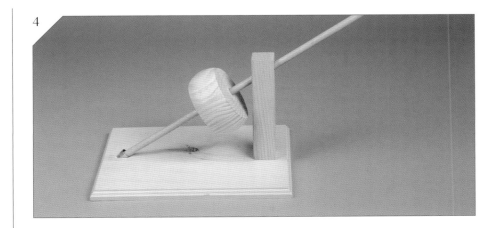

4

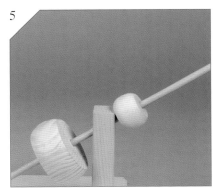

5

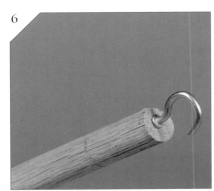

6

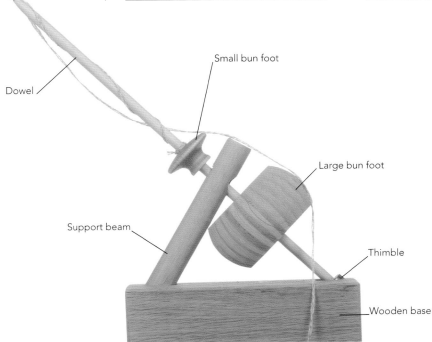

Hook

Dowel

Small bun foot

Large bun foot

Support beam

Thimble

Wooden base

Spinning

A kick spindle is a drop spindle that you spin with your feet. This allows both of your hands to be free to handle and control the fiber. A kick spindle is a great halfway point between drop spindling and wheel spinning.

Spinning a single

1 Attach a leader. Loop the thread through the leader thread on your kick spindle. Kick the whorl of the spindle so that it turns toward you.

2 Gently draft the fibers with your fingers while the spindle spins.

3 When you are ready to wind the yarn onto the staff of the kick spindle, stop the spin with your foot and unhook the yarn from the hook. Then gently kick the whorl and twist the yarn around the base of the spindle. Hook the yarn onto the hook of the spindle and continue spinning.

Materials
Kick spindle | Fiber prepared for spinning (any roving, top, or batt)

+ Place the kick spindle at your feet. Use your foot to gently spin the whorl at the bottom of the spindle. This will create the twist you need to spin yarn. Other than using your foot to spin the spindle, the dynamics of using a kick spindle and a drop spindle are the same.

1

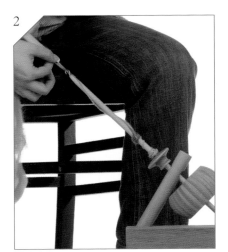

2

3

Spinning a thick and thin single

1 Loop the thread through the leader thread on your kick spindle. Kick the whorl of the spindle so that it turns toward you. Gently draft the fibers with your fingers while the spindle spins. When you want to create a thick spot in your yarn, pinch a large section of fiber and twist your wrist so your thumb keeps the fiber tight.

2 Pull a large chunk of fiber and slide your front hand backward over this thick section to allow the twist to cover it. Draft backward carefully to create a thinner section of yarn after the thick section. Create thick and thin sections at random or at regular intervals for unique knitting and crochet effects.

3 When you are ready to wind the yarn onto the staff of the kick spindle, stop the spin with your foot and unhook the yarn from the hook. Gently kick the whorl and twist the yarn around the base of the spindle. Hook the yarn onto the hook of the spindle and continue spinning.

1

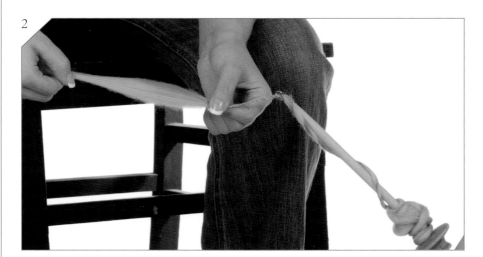

2

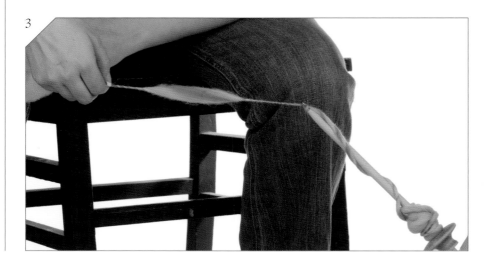

3

Corespinning

Corespinning creates a warmer yarn for next-to-skin knits. Or try spinning with a novelty thread as the core (eyelash, bouclé, etc.) for a unique art yarn for knitting or crochet.

1 Tie your core thread into a knot and loop it through the leader thread on your kick spindle. Kick the whorl of the spindle so that it turns toward you.

2 Gently draft the fibers with your fingers at a 90-degree angle, wrapping around the core thread while the spindle spins.

3 When you are ready to wind the yarn onto the staff of the kick spindle, stop the spin with your foot and unhook the yarn from the hook. Gently kick the whorl and twist the yarn around the base of the spindle. Hook the yarn onto the hook of the spindle and continue spinning.

+

The core of your yarn will determine its "personality." If you use a crochet cotton core, the yarn will drape like crochet cotton. Many spinners prefer using a wool core, or a core that is the same fiber as what they are spinning around it. Try using different core threads and see what works best for you. Novelty yarns such as eyelash and bouclé are fun to corespin, and so are elastic and hemp.

Materials
Kick spindle | Strong core thread | Fiber prepared for spinning (blended or art batt)

1

2

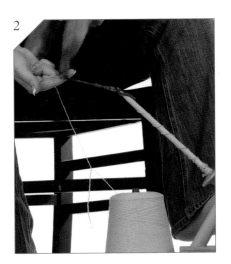

3

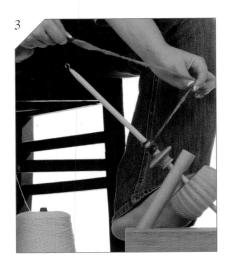

Plying

Many spinners find that plying is easier than spinning. You can practice plying using commercially spun yarns and thread. Plying the yarn upon itself is a very traditional way to create a stable, soft yarn for knitting or crochet.

1 Tie the ends of your handspun single in a knot and loop it through the leader thread on your kick spindle.

2 Kick the whorl of the spindle so that it turns away from you. Allow the yarn to twist upon itself, creating a two-ply yarn.

3 To ply a yarn with thread, knot the single yarn with the plying thread and loop it through the leader thread of your kick spindle.

4 Kick the whorl of the spindle so that it turns away from you. Allow the plying thread and the yarn to twist against each other. When you are ready to wind the yarn onto the staff of the kick spindle, stop the spin with your foot and unhook the yarn. Gently kick the whorl and twist the yarn around the base of the spindle. To continue spinning, hook the yarn onto the hook of the spindle, and carry on. Make sure you always kick the whorl away from you.

Materials
Kick spindle | Handspun single-ply yarn | Strong plying thread

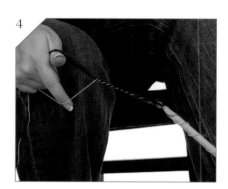

+

You can ply two handspun yarns together, or ply a handspun single yarn with a commercial yarn. Or try plying three or four yarns together to create a bulky yarn. Plying the yarn with a thread (see page 106) can create unique and artistic textures and effects. The possibilities are endless!

Fancy Plying

You can create many different textures and effects in your yarn, simply by changing the angle at which you ply. Try plying a thick and thin handspun yarn to create "bubbles," or a self-striping yarn to create coils. Experiment and see what you can create.

1 Tie your plying thread and fiber into a knot and loop it through the leader thread on your kick spindle. Kick the whorl of the spindle so that it turns away from you. Allow the plying thread and the yarn to twist against each other, creating the ply.

2 **Bubble ply** Hold your yarn and plying thread at a 45-degree angle to each other to create a bubbly effect in the plied yarn.

Coil ply (shown in photo) Hold your yarn and plying thread at a 90-degree angle to each other to create a coil effect in your plied yarn. For a tighter coil, push the yarn up the plying thread. Make sure you choose a strong plying thread for this method so that your yarn has integrity.

Shell ply Start by using a thick-and-thin single yarn. The thick sections of the yarn will be the "shells" in your finished plied yarn. Hold your yarn and plying thread at a 45-degree angle to each other as you begin. When you reach a thick section of yarn, hold the yarn at a 90-degree angle to the plying thread. For a rounder shell shape, push the yarn up the plying thread. Make sure you choose a strong plying thread for this method so that your yarn has integrity.

Materials
Kick spindle | Handspun single-ply yarn | Strong plying thread

1

2

3 When you are ready to wind the yarn onto the staff of the kick spindle, stop the spin with your foot and unhook the yarn from the hook. Then gently kick the whorl and twist the yarn around the base of the spindle.

4 To continue, hook the yarn onto the hook of the spindle and carry on spinning. Make sure that, when plying, you always kick the direction of the whorl away from you.

Thread Wrapping

Add a little sparkle to your single ply yarn by adding a wrap of metallic thread, or try using a commercial mohair yarn to add a fuzzy halo wrap to your single. This is a great way to add texture to your yarn while spinning it in just one step.

1 Take a spool or cone of thread and place it on the floor next to your kick spindle. Then tie the thread into a knot with the beginning of your fiber. Place this knot into the loop of your leader thread and kick the whorl of the spindle so that it turns toward you, creating twist.

2 While holding the wrapping thread in your hand, gently draft the fibers with your fingers while the spindle spins. This will wrap the thread around the yarn, creating a beautiful barber pole effect. For different effects try using multiple strands of thread or novelty yarns as your thread wrap. Commercial mohair creates a beautiful thread-wrap "halo" around the yarn.

Materials
Kick spindle | Fiber prepared for spinning (any roving, top, or batt) | Fine thread for wrapping

1

2

+ Want to add more texture? Try plying your yarn after thread wrapping it! See pages 104–105 for different plying techniques.

3 When you have spun a long length of yarn and want to wind the yarn onto the staff of the kick spindle, stop the spin with your foot and unhook the yarn from the hook. Then gently kick the whorl and twist the yarn around the base of the spindle. Hook the yarn onto the hook of the spindle and continue spinning.

3

Mixed Media: Spinning Beads into a Single

Spinning beads into yarn makes a fun embellishment skein to include in your projects. You can spin large beads into your yarn using this technique. For smaller beads, see the "Plying Beads into a Single" directions on page 110.

1 Prepare your beads by threading wool through the holes using a large-eyed needle.

2 Spin a length of single yarn (see pages 100–101), at least one yard before you add the first bead.

Materials

Kick spindle | Beads with large holes or other add-ins | Large-eyed needle (make sure this needle will fit through your beads or other add-ins) | Fiber prepared for spinning (any roving, top, or batt)

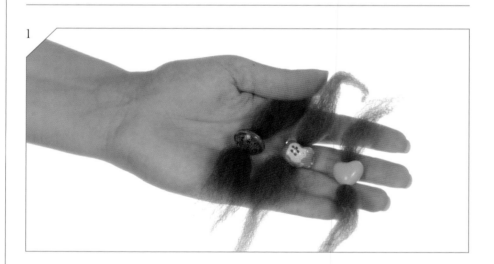

1

2

+ After the bead is spun into the yarn, it may slide up and down the yarn depending on how fine you are spinning and how large the hole of the bead is. When you are knitting, weaving, or crocheting the yarn you can slide the bead to the front of your work, so it doesn't get hidden on the inside or back of your finished item.

3 Attach the fibers from one side of the bead to the single by pinching the ends together with your fingers and then kicking the whorl of the wheel to allow the twist to travel up the fibers.

4 Attach the rest of the wool in the bead back to your fiber and continue spinning until you want to add the next bead. When you are ready to wind the yarn onto the staff of the spindle, stop the spin with your foot and unhook the yarn. Gently kick the whorl and twist the yarn around the base of the spindle. To continue spinning, hook the yarn onto the hook of the spindle and carry on.

3

4

Mixed Media: Plying Beads into a Single

For smaller beads, or beads with smaller holes, try plying them into your handspun single. First you will need to spin a single yarn (see pages 100–101), and you'll also need to choose a plying thread that won't break under the weight of the beads.

1 Begin by threading your beads onto your plying thread. Make sure you choose a plying thread that is strong enough to resist breaking if it is put under tension. Tie your plying thread and yarn into a knot and loop it through the leader thread on your kick spindle. Kick the whorl of the spindle so that it turns away from you. Allow the plying thread and the yarn to twist against each other, creating the ply.

Materials

Kick spindle | Beads or other add-ins | Strong plying thread (make sure the beads or add-ins you are using can be strung on your plying thread, and that this thread does not break easily) | Fiber prepared for spinning (any roving, top, or batt)

1

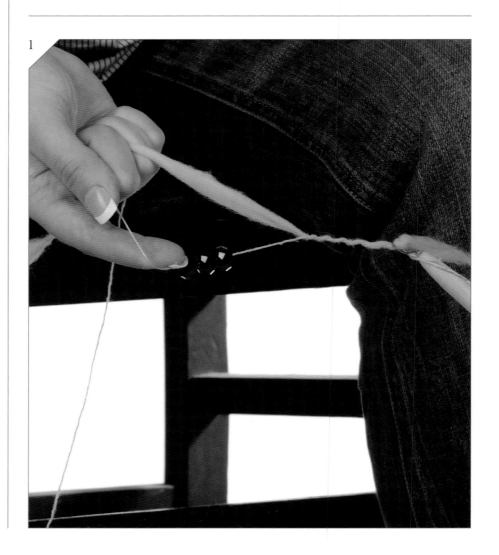

Try spinning larger beads for a more dramatic effect in your yarn. Or spin clusters of smaller beads into your yarn. You can also mix and match large beads with smaller beads. Beaded skeins are beautiful just as they are, worn like a necklace or cowl.

2   When you want to add a bead, bring a bead up from your plying thread and wrap it around your yarn as you are plying. Light beads work best for this process, as very heavy beads will cause the thread to sag.

3   To continue plying after you have added a bead, hook the yarn onto the hook of the spindle. Make sure that, when plying, you always kick the direction of the whorl away from you.

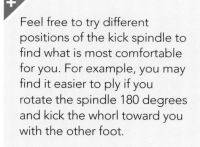

Feel free to try different positions of the kick spindle to find what is most comfortable for you. For example, you may find it easier to ply if you rotate the spindle 180 degrees and kick the whorl toward you with the other foot.

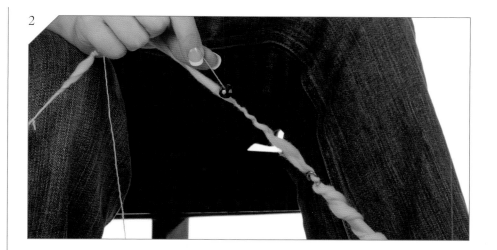

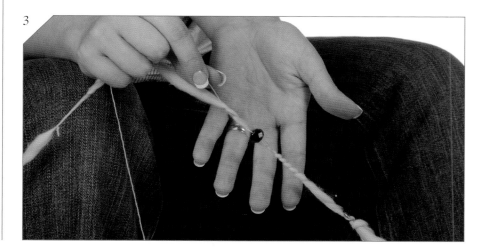

Gallery

Drop Spun Yarns

Opposite: Three-ply yarn by Brittany Wilson of BoHo Knitter Chic
Top: Handspun yarn by Renae Scartabello of TerraBellaSpun
Bottom left: Single yarn by Ashley Martineau of Neauveau Fiber Arts
Bottom right: Yarn by Kristine Haddock of Storybook Fibers

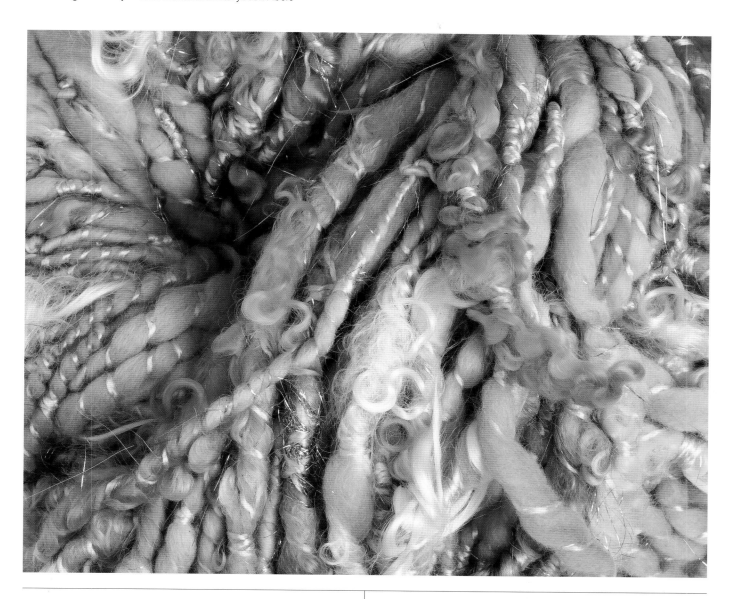

Above: Drop spun yarns by Kristine Haddock of Storybook Fibers
Opposite: Shellspun yarn by Ashley Martineau of Neauveau Fiber Arts

Top: Handspun bubble plied yarn by Ashley Martineau of Neauveau Fiber Arts
Right: Corespun yarn by Allison Jai
Opposite: Coiled yarn by Jessie Driscoll of Stash Enhancement

Michelle Snowdon

Michelle seeks inspiration from her own handspun yarn to create expressive wearable designs and artworks. By improvising with traditional techniques, Michelle creates innovative, cutting-edge yarn and neckwear designs right on the wheel. Process is a key element in Michelle's unique design practice. She explores a multilayering of novelty spinning techniques, one of her favorites being "Navajo the Navajo," to achieve six- and nine-plied cables, ready to wear off the bobbin.

Michelle refers to her process as "freestyle spinning," in a reference to the free-form movements across the media of knit, crochet and Saori weaving. She says: "Handspun yarn is an inspiring material. As a raw form it is full of vitality and potential. I am continuously exploring twist energy and trying to push my own boundaries with technique. The new-wave handspinning movement affirms handspun yarn as a finished item, not merely as a supply to be worked further. The paradigm is shifting, and it is exciting to connect with the global community of spinners who enjoy stretching the boundaries of what is possible with handspun."

"It is exciting to connect with the global community of spinners who enjoy stretching the boundaries of what is possible with handspun."

Freestyle spinning produces yarn that is lively and fresh, awakened in character and form. It builds on the notions of art yarn and novelty yarn, whereby techniques are explored, juxtaposed, and refined. Design elements, such as color, composition, and movement along the length of the yarn are considered. Michelle's yarns are a tactile artistic response to her photographic explorations. Ideas are articulated initially as batts, then as skeins of handspun yarn through a carefully selected palette of materials, which she dyes and blends in her home studio. These expressive yarns hold their own story—they become landscapes, waterfalls, flora, and poetry.

"This process is creatively freeing, perfect for awakening creative flow."

"With freestyle spinning we begin with the intention to observe the interplay between self, materials, threads, and wheel, and to be attentive to the forming yarn. Spontaneous movements and gestures are captured as sketches into the twisting thread. The end result is a dynamic sculptural form, a 3-D rendition filled with texture and personality. These yarns are highly functional. I might weave one on a giant handmade loom, create string art, drape it as a garland, or make an infinity scarf. There is much potential for keeping the yarn intact and true, without hiding the beautiful passages in loops and knots. This process is creatively freeing, perfect for awakening creative flow." Michelle is often sought out to teach this method to new students and to those who are returning to the craft seeking renewed inspiration.

Michelle's fiber hopes and dreams are to keep making and exploring the medium, to grow her career as a fiber artist, and to continue to teach. It is to be hoped that public education in fiber arts can be fostered, allowing emerging fiber artists, craft artisans, and wool growers to share skills and resources, be inspired to innovate and collaborate, and evolve the art of handspinning.

Opposite: Textured art yarn corespun with various wools and wool locks, shredded silks, and threads
Top left: Yarn spun from dyed wools, natural fibers, and wooden beads. Spun thick and thin as a single, and then Navajo plied
Top right: Yarn spun from hand-painted wool top in an extreme thick and thin style, then plied using the bubble ply technique on page 144

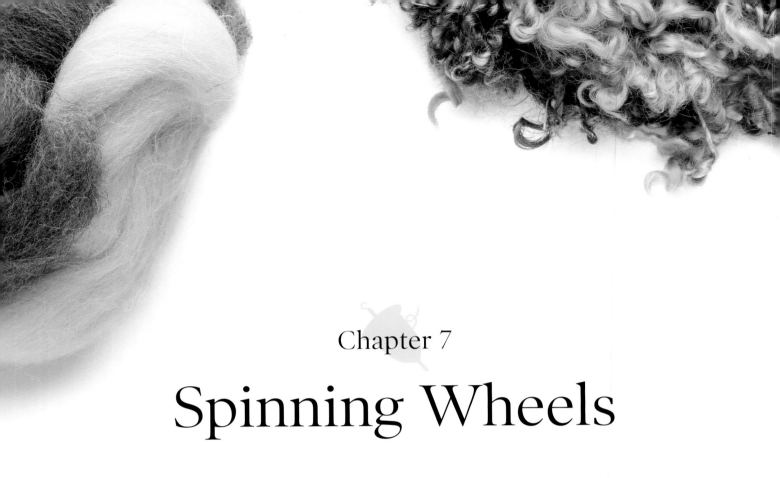

Chapter 7

Spinning Wheels

This section covers multiple traditional techniques, as well as a few playful "art yarn" techniques you can experiment with to create one-of-a-kind skeins of yarn for embellishments, weavings, and free-form crochet. Also included in this chapter are instructions for building your own spinning wheel. Try combining different techniques and building one technique upon another to create unique textured yarns. The possibilities are endless.

Troubleshooting Tips

Problem: My wheel won't bring the yarn onto the bobbin (uptake).
Solution: Increase the tension on the wheel and make sure the yarn isn't caught on the hooks on the flyer.

Problem: My wheel pulls the yarn onto the bobbin so quickly that my yarn breaks, or the fibers don't have a chance to spin.
Solution: Decrease the tension on the wheel.

Problem: My yarn is overtwisted.
Solution: Either your ratio is too high (your bobbin is spinning too fast and putting too much twist into your yarn) or your tension is too low. Try spinning at a lower ratio or increasing the tension so the yarn goes onto the bobbin before it becomes overtwisted. Or consider that you may be holding onto the fiber for too long. Relax your hands and allow the yarn to go into the bobbin before it becomes overtwisted.

Problem: When I ply my yarn it falls apart or twists upon itself.
Solution: Make sure you put plenty of twist into your yarn before plying to prevent it from falling apart. If twist is not an issue, then you are plying in the wrong direction. This means you are trying to ply the yarn in the same direction in which it has been spun.

In order to ply correctly, you need to ply the yarn in the opposite direction than it has been spun. The easiest way to prevent this problem is to develop the habit of always spinning your singles in a clockwise direction, and always plying in a counterclockwise direction.

Problem: My yarn keeps getting caught on the flyer hooks.
Solution: Consider replacing the hooks on your flyer with L-hooks. L-hooks are shaped like the letter "L" and often don't catch on yarns like traditional hooks do. You can also use pliers to open the hooks on your flyer to allow the yarn to pass through freely.

Problem: I want to buy a spinning wheel, but I don't know how to choose.
Solution: Test-drive multiple wheels before you buy. Find a wheel that is comfortable for you to spin on. Also consider the type of yarn you want to spin (traditional, textured, art) and the purpose of the yarn you're spinning (socks, sweaters, rugs, blankets). Make sure the orifice is large enough for the yarn you want to spin (bulky spinners prefer a 1-inch/2.5-cm or larger orifice) and the bobbin is large enough for the yardage you will need for your projects (or invest in multiple bobbins).

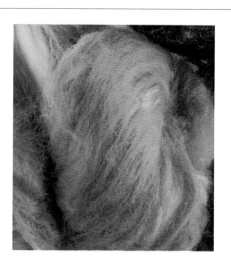

Opposite, clockwise from top left: Natural and white wool top; yarn spun from dyed wool locks; pulled roving by Elizabeth Stottlemeyer
Far left: Commercial top blends of wool and alpaca fiber
Left: Pulled roving by Elizabeth Stottlemeyer

Choosing a Spinning Wheel

You'll need to think about what kind of yarn you'd like to spin: traditional or textured? Then consider what the very finest yarn you'll want to spin is: very fine, somewhat fine, or worsted? And the bulkiest you'll want to go: worsted, chunky, or even bulky?

Finally, think about the kinds of projects you'll be making with your handspun yarn. Big projects, that require a lot of yardage? A mix of projects—some big and some small? Or mostly smaller projects such as mittens, hats, and socks?

There are five main areas of the spinning wheel that you'll need to make decisions about, based on your answers to the questions above.

Drive

Many traditional spinners prefer a double-drive wheel, which helps them spin consistent, repeatable yarns. Art yarn spinners often prefer a single-drive wheel, which is easier to adjust and allows for creation of a greater range of yarns.

There are two types of single-drive wheel: the Irish tension/bobbin-led kind, which is better for medium to super bulky yarns; and the Scotch tension/flyer-led kind, which is better for finer yarns of the two, though is also able to manage bulky yarns with the right ratios.

Each wheel is a tool for spinning a certain range and type of yarn. There is no one perfect wheel, but there is a perfect wheel for you and the yarn you want to spin. Try asking spinners why they chose their wheel(s), and spin on different wheels before you buy.

Ratios

If you want to spin very fine yarn, look at the ratios. Ratios determine how fast the bobbin and flyer spin. A faster spin creates more twist and a finer yarn. For fine yarns, you want a high ratio. A wheel with lower ratios works best for spinning bulky yarns.

Orifice

If you are planning on spinning yarns finer than a chunky worsted weight, any size of orifice will work for you. But if you're wanting bulky yarns, look for an orifice over 1 inch (2.5 cm), a hook orifice, a delta orifice, or a by-passable orifice. Flyers with small hooks will often trap or catch on bulky or textured yarns. Look at where the yarn needs to travel from the orifice to the bobbin to make sure there is adequate space for the kind of yarn you want to spin.

Bobbin

If you spin bulky yarn on a small bobbin, you will be limited to 30–60 yards (27–55 m) per bobbin. Some wheels have a jumbo flyer package you can add to your wheel to get more yardage and bulkier yarn. If you spin fine yarn, the bobbin size won't be as limiting. If you will be making large projects out of fine yarn, you may want to consider purchasing extra bobbins to suit the yardage you require.

Treadles

Wheels come in single- and double-treadle versions, with the treadles being the foot pedal part. Single-treadle is more budget-friendly, while double-treadle is usually more ergonomic, so decide which works better for you.

Opposite: The Ashford Country Spinner spinning wheel. A wheel like this is a good choice if you want to spin a lot of yardage or very bulky yarns with big embellishments
Inset 1: Note the large orifice on this wheel. Although not ideal for fine-weight yarns, worsted weight to super bulky yarns can be spun easily on this kind of wheel
Inset 2: Note the large bobbin on this wheel. It is ideal for spinning up large amounts of yardage for big projects

Bobbin

Flyer

Drive band

Orifice

1

2

Footman
(behind the
wheel)

Treadles

Building a Spinning Wheel

This simple spinning wheel can be built with minimal experience, using simple tools and equipment available from hardware and craft stores. You can find out more about building spinning wheels, as well as modifications, improvements, supplements, replacement parts, and other ideas, in spinning communities online—try the DIY Wheels Group on Ravelry (www.ravelry.com).

Tools
PVC cutting tool | Screwdriver | Adjustable wrench | Circular saw

Materials
Pieces required: You may need to adjust the size of some of the following pieces, based on what is available in your area and the size of wheel you end up using. Please read the assembly instructions before purchasing supplies so you can see how the wheel is assembled and make any necessary adjustments to the following list.

1-inch (2.5-cm) diameter PVC pipe pieces (schedule 40):
- 4 x 13 inch (33 cm)
- 8 x 9 inch (23 cm)
- 12 x three-way 90-degree side outlet elbow
- 12 x T pieces
- 1 x 3 inch (7.5 cm)—cut a 1-inch (2.5-cm) diameter hole through it about ½ inch (1.25 cm) from the top
- 1 x 3 inch (7.5 cm)—cut a semicircle into the top, 1¼ inches (3 cm) from side to side
- 2 x 19 inch (48 cm)
- 4 x 5½ inch (14 cm)
- 4 x 3 inch (7.5 cm)
- 1 x 10 inch (25 cm)
- 1 x four-way PVC pipe cross

½-inch (1.25-cm) diameter PVC pipe pieces (schedule 40):
- 1 x 2½-inch (6.5-cm) 1-inch (2.5-cm) diameter
- 1 x 1 inch (2.5 cm) to ½ inch (1.25 cm) diameter bushing
- 1 x 14 inch (36 cm)
- 2 x 10 inch (25 cm)
- 2 x slip to thread 1 inch (2.5 cm) to ½ inch (1.25 cm) elbows

Other hardware required
1 x 13 inch (33 cm) bicycle wheel. Your wheel may have slightly different dimensions; make sure you purchase a correct size bolt to go through the wheel and any holes you need to cut into the PVC pipe to support your wheel. See the wheel assembly instructions to determine the exact size of hardware your wheel will require if it is a size other than 13 inch (33 cm).

- 8 x 1-inch (2.5-cm) cup hooks
- 1 x eye hook screw
- 1 x 2-inch (5-cm) bolt to fit through the eye hook
- 1 x nut that fits the 2-inch (5-cm) bolt
- 1 x piece of 1-inch (2.5-cm) x 6-inch (15-cm) duct tape folded over onto itself
- 1 x small screw
- 1 x 7-inch (18-cm) carriage bolt
- 2 x washers to fit 7-inch (18-cm) carriage bolt
- 4 x nuts that fit on the 7-inch (18-cm) carriage bolt
- 1 x 2-inch (5-cm) metal repair plate
- 2 x 1¼-inch (3-cm) bolts
- 6 x nuts to fit the 1¼-inch (3-cm) bolts
- 1 x 3-inch (7.5-cm) metal repair plate
- 2 x 2½-inch (6-cm) packaged door hinges (with included screws)

Wooden and craft pieces required
- 3 x 4-inch (10-cm) wooden craft circles with a 1¼-inch (3-cm) diameter hole cut through the center, exactly the same as the outside diameter of the 1-inch (2.5-cm) PVC pipe
- 1 x 74-inch (188-cm) leather shoelace (adjust to the size of your wheel as necessary; this size is generous for a 13-inch/33-cm bicycle wheel)
- 2 x pieces of wood suitable for treadles. (We used craft wood cutting boards with drilled holes. You can use any wood pieces less than ½ inch (1.25 cm) thick, 4 inches (10 cm) wide, and 7 inches (18 cm) long
- 2 x 20-inch (50-cm) leather shoelaces

Building the frame of the wheel

1 Assemble the base of the wheel using a two 13-inch (33-cm) piece in front (where the treadles will attach) and the two 9-inch (23-cm) pieces behind, attached by two three-way 90-degree side outlet elbow pieces. Then, using T-pieces, attach to each 9-inch (23-cm) piece and 3-inch (7.5-cm) piece. The back of the wheel will be another piece of 13-inch (33-cm) piping, attached by two three-way 90-degree side outlet elbow pieces.

2 Place four 9-inch (23-cm) pieces vertically into the two center T-pieces and the two 90-degree three-way elbows of the base. Place the two 19-inch (48-cm) pieces into the front three-way elbows of the wheel base.

3 Drill a hole in the center of the two 13-inch (33-cm) pieces in the center. The hole drilled here was ⅜ inch (1 cm) in diameter, to fit the bolt that went through the bicycle wheel. You may need a different-sized hole depending on the bicycle wheel you use. Drill a hole to fit the bolt that will run through the wheel and be supported by these two pieces of PVC pipe.

4 **(a and b)** Place the four T-pieces on the back and the center PVC pipe pieces, standing vertically. Place the two 13-inch (33-cm) pieces with the drilled holes between the T-pieces.

1
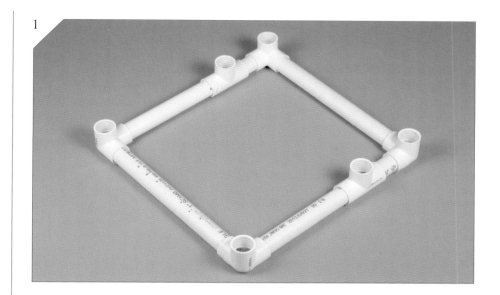

2
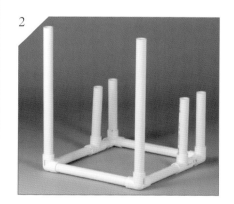

3
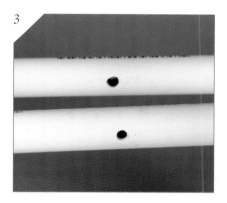

4a
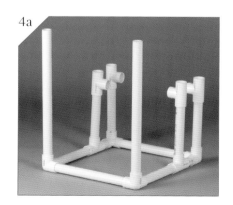

4b

Continues on next page

Assembling the top of the frame

5 **(a–c)** Place the four 9-inch (23-cm) pieces vertically into the center and back T-pieces. Place the four three-way 90-degree corners into the front and back corners of the wheel frame. Place the two T-pieces into the two central vertical pieces. Place two 5½-inch (14-cm) pieces into the front and back of the frame, using an upside-down T-piece to secure them. Place the two 3-inch (7.5-cm) pieces into the back three-way 90-degree corners. Secure with the T-piece. Place the final two 5½-inch (14-cm) pieces into the T-piece toward the front, and secure with a 90-degree corner.

Assembling the flyer support

6 **(a and b)** Place the 3-inch (7.5-cm) piece with a 1-inch (2.5-cm) diameter hole cut through it into the back upside-down T-piece. Place the 3-inch (7.5-cm) piece with the semicircle (diameter 1¼ inches/3 cm) cut through the top into the front upside-down T.

5a

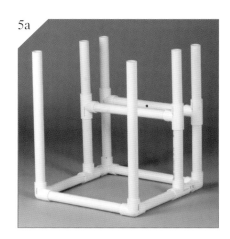

5b

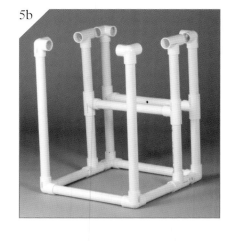

5c

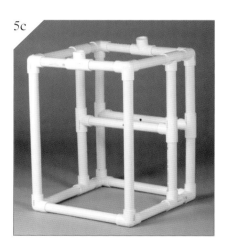

6a

6b

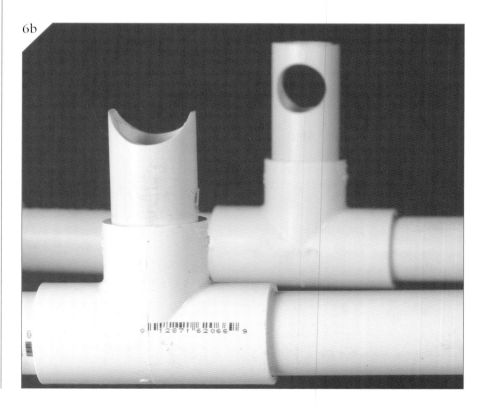

Assembling the flyer

7 The flyer is made using the ½-inch (1.25-cm) PVC pieces.

8 **(a and b)** Place the 2½-inch (6.5-cm) 1-inch (2.5-cm) diameter PVC pipe into the four-way PVC 1-inch (2.5-cm) cross piece with the hole cut into the middle. Place the 1 inch (2.5 cm) to ½ inch (1.25 cm) bushing into the front of the four-way PVC pipe cross. Place the 14-inch (36-cm), ½-inch (1.25-cm) PVC pipe into the bushing. Screw the two male thread elbows into those bushings. Insert the 10-inch (25-cm) ½-inch (1.25-cm) diameter piece. Repeat for the other side of the flyer. Insert the eight 1-inch (2.5-cm) hooks, four on each side of the flyer arms.

7

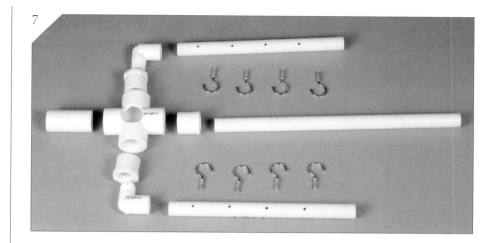

8a

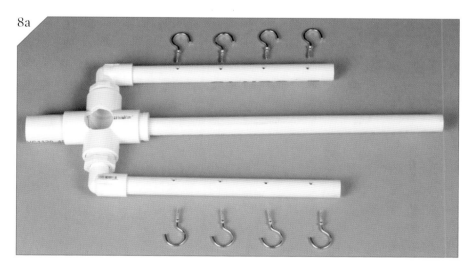

8b

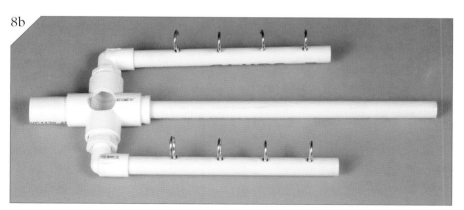

Continues on next page

9 Place the flyer onto the wheel base. Place the long center portion of the flyer through the hole in the rear flyer support. Rest the flyer onto the semi-circle cut into the front PVC pipe. This will be your orifice.

Assembling the bobbins

You may assemble multiple bobbins for this wheel.

10 Glue two of the 3–4-inch (7.5–10-cm) craft circles back to back to create a ridge for the drive band to go over. Place the front craft circle at the front of the bobbin with the base facing the back of the bobbin.

11 Carefully slide the bobbin onto the long center arm of the flyer from front to back so the drive band will go over the groove in the bobbin and around the bicycle wheel.

9

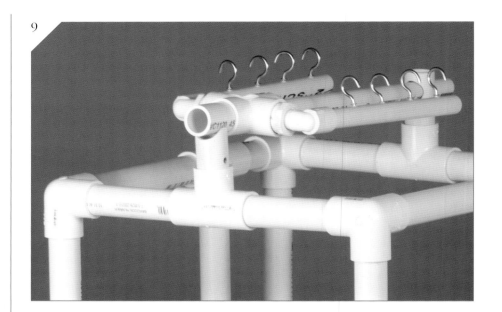

10

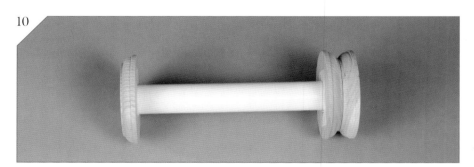

11

Assembling the tension knob

12 **(a and b)** Screw the eye hook into the left side of the top front flyer half-circle piece. Screw the duct tape onto the right side of the flyer support. Place the duct tape over the orifice of the flyer and cut a hole into it. Slide the 2-inch (5-cm) bolt through the hole and place the bolt into the eye of the eye hook. Use the nut to secure the bolt. Note: This wheel does not require a lot of tension to spin—in fact, you may not need much tension at all, but this option allows you to adjust it.

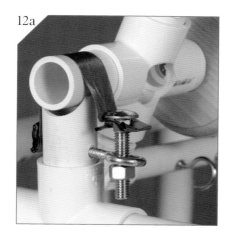

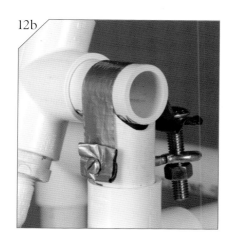

Attaching the wheel to the base

13 Place the 7-inch (18-cm) carriage bolt through the back of the wheel and through the first PVC pipe. Put a nut and a washer onto this bolt from back to front. The washers touch the bicycle wheel and the nuts touch the PVC pipe.

14 Place the bicycle wheel onto the bolt and add another washer and another nut. Continue screwing the bolt through the PVC pipe support system of the wheel until it is secure. Once the bolt is through the PVC pipe support system, tighten the nuts around the bicycle wheel. This will help balance and stabilize the bicycle wheel, preventing wobbling during use. Use an adjustable wrench to tighten all the nuts.

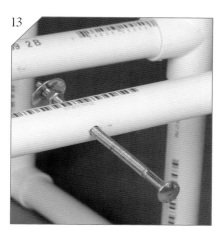

Assembling the footman-to-wheel connection

15 Screw another nut onto the carriage bolt coming through the PVC pipe. Add the 2-inch (5-cm) metal repair piece to the bolt. Screw a nut onto the bolt and tighten it around the metal repair plate.

16 Place a 1¼-inch (3-cm) bolt through the empty hole of the metal repair plate, pointing away from the wheel. Add a nut and secure tightly.

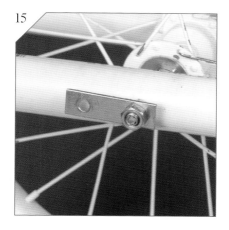

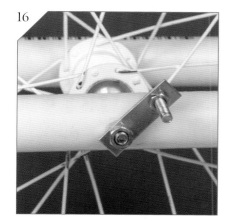

Continues on next page

17 Add a nut to the bolt, leaving it near the end. Add the 3-inch (7.5-cm) metal repair plate. Add another nut and tighten.

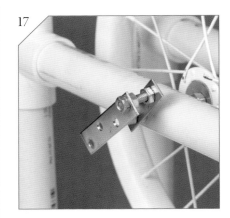

18 Add a nut to the 1¼-inch (3-cm) bolt. Slide the bolt through the fourth (farthest) empty hole of the 3-inch (7.5-cm) metal repair plate. Add a nut to the bolt and tighten to secure. Finish by adding a second nut to the bolt for extra security.

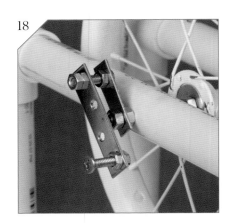

Assembling the treadles

19 Choose where your hinges are screwed into the PVC based on the wooden treadle pieces you have purchased. Screw the door hinges into the base PVC pipe. Screw the hinges into the base of the treadles.

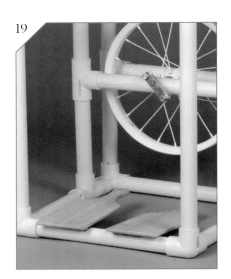

Attaching the treadles to the footman

20 With the long repair metal piece facing to the left, tie a 20-inch (50-cm) leather shoelace through the hole of the left treadle and then loosely tie it around the last 1¼-inch (3-cm) bolt that was attached.

Assemble the right-hand treadle by tying the other leather shoelace through the hole of the right treadle and onto the first bolt of the footman assembly.

Attaching the drive band

21 Take the 74-inch (188-cm) leather shoelace and wrap it around the bicycle wheel and onto the bobbin. Tie it into a square knot securely but not too tightly. Trim the leather pieces of the treadles and drive band to fit. Tighten any nuts or bolts as necessary to help your wheel spin smoothly.

22 Your spinning wheel is now complete and ready to use.

22

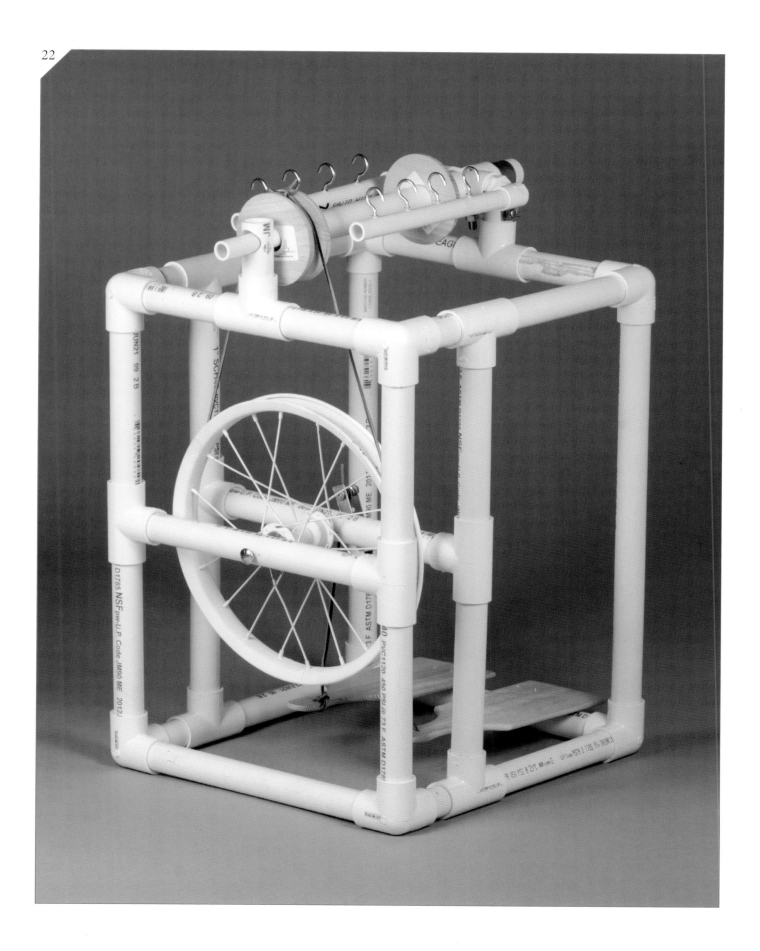

Spinning a Thick and Thin Single

With your leader thread fed through the orifice, take some of your fiber and loop it through the leader thread loop. Treadle your wheel in a clockwise direction. As you see the twist traveling up the loop and into the fiber, pinch and pull more fiber forward and slide your fingers back as the twist continues up the fiber. This process of pinching and pulling the fiber is called drafting. The size of the yarn is determined by how much fiber is drafted and twisted. Draft a small amount of fiber to spin a thin yarn, and a large amount of fiber to spin a bulky yarn.

1 Once you have mastered both the woolen and worsted techniques, you can use a combination of them to create a repeatable thick and thin single. Begin spinning using the woolen drafting method.

2 Pinch a large section of fiber with your thumb and pull forward.

Materials
Spinning wheel | Several cones or spools of spinning fiber—include at least one mohair thread | One strong core thread or handspun single-ply yarn

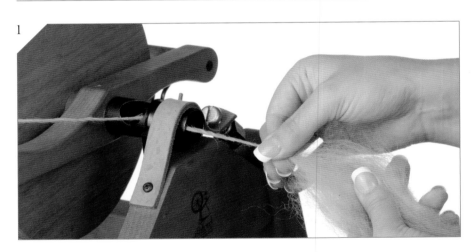

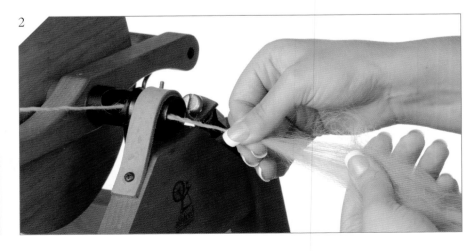

3 Slide your front hand backward over that large section of fiber.

4 Do two worsted (backward) drafts.

5 Give the yarn to the wheel and do two woolen (forward) drafts. To achieve a consistent thick and thin single, repeat the number of worsted drafts and woolen drafts between each pinch of fiber. For a more random thick and thin yarn, do a random number of worsted and woolen drafts.

+

The challenge is making sure you do not allow the twist to travel behind your front hand. This will put twist in all the fiber you have to spin and make it very difficult to draft. If you end up with twist in your fiber, stop treading and take a moment to untwist the fiber in the opposite direction.

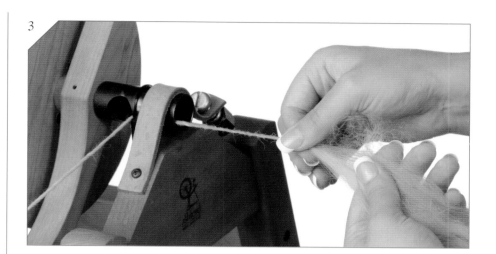

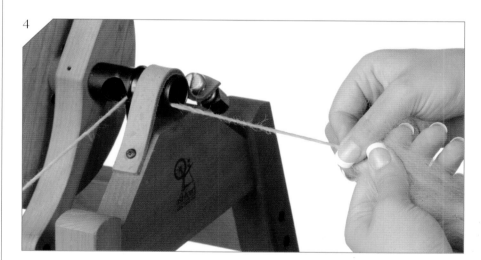

Spinning Locks

You can spin locks with very little preparation. Simply take a handful of wool locks and fluff them into a cloud of wool with your fingers. This is called hand picking. The more you pick the wool, the easier it will be to spin. Make sure to leave some curly tips to give the yarn that fresh-off-the-sheep look.

1 Loop a section of wool locks through the leader thread in the orifice. Begin treadling and spinning the yarn in a clockwise direction.

2 **(a)** As the twist travels up the fiber, use a woolen (forward) draft to separate the locks as you spin.

(b) This creates a chunky, curly-textured yarn.

Materials
Spinning wheel | Natural or dyed wool or mohair locks

1

2a

2b

Try experimenting with different fibers, threads, and embellishments (feathers, sparkles, sequins, buttons, and beads) to create unique skeins

Corespinning Wire

Corespinning wire is very similar to corespinning yarn, but with one extra consideration: wire cannot accumulate twist, so it must be able to spin freely to release the twist during spinning. Use wirespun yarn for jewelry, knit and crochet projects, weaving, basket making, purse handles, home décor, and gift wrap.

1 Remove the lid and place the spool of wire in the plastic container. Thread the wire through a hole in the lid or container. Pull out some wire from the spool so that it hangs freely above the floor.

2 Loop the wire through the leader thread loop in the orifice.

3 Begin spinning. Treat the wire as the core and guide the wool around the wire at a 90-degree angle while spinning, allowing the wire to spin freely between your feet.

4 As you approach the end of the wire, remove it from the container. Bend the end of the wire back on itself. Spin over both pieces to finish.

Materials

Spinning wheel | Small plastic container with lid | Safety pin or thumbtack | 26-gauge wire (beading, floral, or copper wire) on a spool | Prepared fiber for spinning (art batts work well)

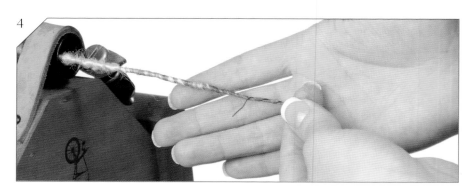

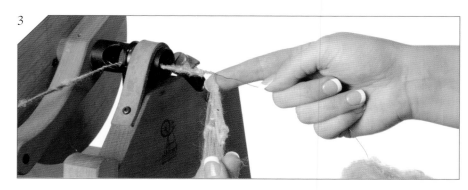

Corespinning Batts

Corespinning is a fun way to get more yardage from a small amount of fiber. In this tutorial you will find out how to corespin an art batt. First, you will need to choose a core for your yarn, which will determine its characteristics.

1 Take the core thread and loop it through the leader thread in the orifice. Spin in a clockwise direction and allow the twist to travel up the core thread to secure it. Take a small amount of fiber and hold it to the core at a 90-degree angle while you are spinning. Allow the fiber to wrap around the core.

2 If you use a smaller amount of fiber, you can spin a finer yarn. A larger amount of fiber will result in a bulkier yarn. Using a fine core thread will also help you create a fine yarn with plenty of drape, whereas a core thread of bulky wool will create a very bulky yarn.

+ Try using different core threads and see what works best for you. Novelty yarns such as eyelash and bouclé are fun to corespin, as are wire (see page 136) and hemp.

Materials
Spinning wheel | Strong core thread | Prepared fiber for spinning (blended batts and art batts work best)

1

2

Fancy Corespinning

If you have a core thread that you want to show off, you can rotate it around the yarn while corespinning for a fun effect.

1 Take the core thread and loop it through the leader thread in the orifice. Spin in a clockwise direction and allow the twist to travel up the core thread to secure it. Take a small amount of fiber and hold it to the core at a 90-degree angle. Allow the fiber to wrap around the core, as with corespinning (see page 137).

2 When you want to show off the core fiber, switch hands. Hold the core thread and fiber in opposite hands from when you started. Wrap the core around the drafted fiber at a 90-degree angle for a section, then switch hands again and wrap the fiber around the core.

3 Continue rotating the fiber on the outside of the core, and the core on the outside of the fiber. You can do this at regular intervals for a self-striping effect, or at random intervals. Try using different core threads for different effects.

Materials

Spinning wheel | Strong novelty core thread (try a bouclé or eyelash yarn for a fun texture) | Prepared fiber for spinning: blended or art batts work best

1

2

3

Yarn by Lexi Boeger of Pluckyfluff

Corespinning Locks

In this tutorial you will find out how to corespin wool locks. As before, you will need to choose a core for your yarn to determine its characteristics.

1 Begin by looping the core thread through the leader loop in the orifice. Spin in a clockwise direction and allow the twist to travel into the core thread to secure.

2 (a) Hold a small amount of locks at a 90-degree angle to the core thread and allow them to wrap around the core thread.

(b) Continue wrapping the picked locks around the core thread for a bulky and super-curly yarn.

Materials
Spinning wheel | Strong core thread | Wool locks

1

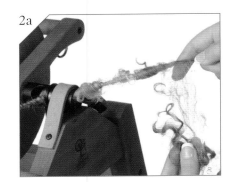

2a

2b

+ Begin by hand picking your locks. Then choose a strong core thread with some texture that will allow the locks to "grab" onto the thread. A smooth core thread will be too slippery and the locks may slide off after spinning. Try using a commercial mohair core thread when corespinning locks.

Thread Wrapping

This is a fun way to add some color or sparkle to your yarn. Choose a thread that contrasts with the fiber you are planning to spin, keeping in mind that the thread you choose to wrap may change the texture of the yarn you're spinning. Fine threads and soft threads are best for yarns that will be worn next to the skin.

1 Place the cone of thread at your feet or on your lazy kate—this will hold it in place as you work. Loop the thread and the fiber through the leader thread loop in the orifice, and begin spinning in a clockwise direction. You may want to begin by holding both the fiber and the thread in one hand once you have spun a length of yarn to the bobbin.

2 Drop the thread, and it will automatically wrap around the yarn you are spinning and add a fun contrasting color to the yarn.

3 Some orifices (hook, delta) may cause the thread to tangle around the bobbin when wrapping. If you are having difficulty thread wrapping with your orifice, try holding the thread with your pinkie to create the 90-degree angle that wrapping requires.

+

Why use just one thread when you can use two or three? Try different types of threads, from sewing thread, to novelty thread, to fuzzy mohair thread for different textures and effects.

Materials
Spinning wheel | Prepared fiber for spinning (top, roving, or batts) | Fine thread for wrapping around (sewing thread, metallic thread, and mohair all work well)

1
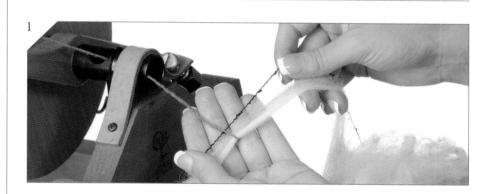

2

3

Plying Basics

Plying is a great way to add texture and balance to your yarn. You can ply the yarn upon itself, another yarn, or a plying thread. Changing the angle at which you ply the yarn will change the texture of the yarn. This section covers several fun ways to ply texture into yarn.

Two-ply basic

1 Take both ends of the yarn and tie them in a knot. Put the knot through the leader thread loop in the orifice and start spinning in a counterclockwise direction.

2 As the twist travels up the ply, slide your fingers back and allow the yarn to ply upon itself.

+ If you want to ply your handspun yarn upon itself, use a ball winder to roll it into a cake. This will prevent it from becoming tangled. Or, you can spin two bobbins of the same fiber and ply them in the same way.

+ Spinning an even yarn will result in an even 2-ply. Spinning a thick and thin yarn will result in a lumpy, bumpy 2-ply. Try spinning different weights of yarn to create different plied textures.

Materials
Spinning wheel | Handspun single-ply yarn

1

2
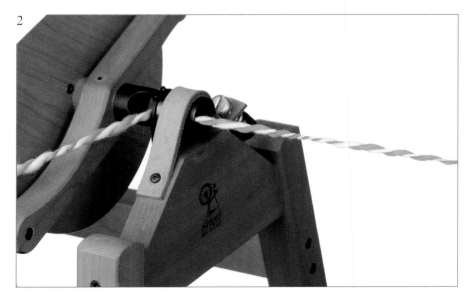

Plying with thread

1 Choose a plying thread that doesn't break easily, and tie it into a knot with your handspun single. Put the knot through the leader thread loop in the orifice and start spinning in a counterclockwise direction.

2 As the twist travels up the ply, slide your fingers back and allow the yarn to be plied by the thread.

+

To create a gentle wave in the ply, hold the thread and the yarn in a "V"-shape with your hands and allow the yarn to go into the orifice gently but quickly.

+

When you ply handspun yarn with thread, the result can be anything from wavy to bubbly.

Materials
Spinning wheel | Handspun single-ply yarn | Strong plying thread

1

2

Plying Bubbles

This technique adds a bit of texture to your yarn without causing you to lose too much yardage. You will get a unique result when you ply a fine single, bulky single, or thick and thin single.

1 Choose a plying thread that doesn't break easily, and tie it in a knot with your handspun single. Put it through the leader thread loop in the orifice and start spinning in a counterclockwise direction. As the twist travels up the ply, slide your fingers back to allow the yarn to be plied by the thread.

2 Hold the yarn at a 70-degree angle to the thread to create a bubbly effect. This is a great technique to use with thick and thin yarns. Allow the yarn to go into the orifice somewhat quickly and before it becomes over twisted.

3 Try this technique on both evenly spun yarn and thick and thin yarn. On an evenly spun yarn, you will get a consistent wavy texture throughout the entire skein. On a yarn that has been spun thick-and-thin, the thicker parts of the yarn will bubble up after plying.

Materials
Spinning wheel | Handspun single-ply yarn | Strong plying thread

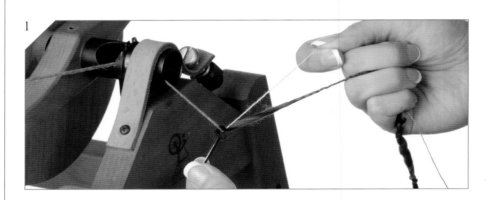
1

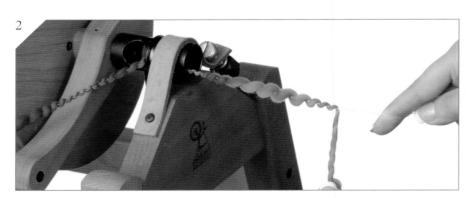
2

3

Plying Coils

For this technique, you will want to choose a very strong plying thread that you will use as a core. Once you master this technique, you won't see the plying thread.

1 **(See Step 1 image on page 144)** Tie the thread in a knot with the handspun single. Put the knot through the leader thread loop in the orifice nd start spinning in a counterclockwise direction. As the twist travels up the ply, slide your fingers back and allow the yarn to be plied by the thread.

2 Hold the yarn at a 90-degree angle to the thread and keep your fingers close together.

3 **(a and b)** As you spin, pause and push the yarn up the thread. Continue spinning at a 90-degree angle, pushing the yarn up the thread. The integrity of the yarn is dependent on the plying thread, so make sure the thread you choose will not break easily. Also, make sure the thread does not have a lot of texture that will prevent you from sliding the yarn up the thread.

Materials
Spinning wheel | Handspun single-ply yarn | Strong plying thread

2
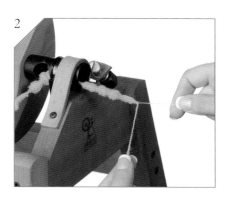

3a
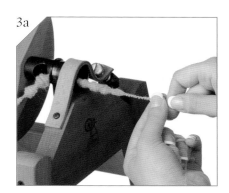

3b
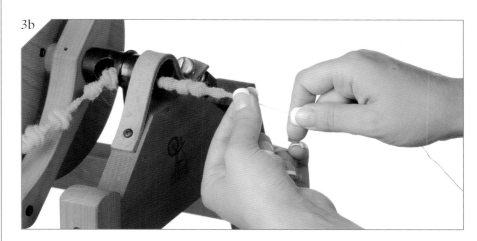

+

This technique uses a lot of yardage—you can estimate that the finished coiled yarn will be about 30 percent of the yardage of the original single. Keep this in mind when you're considering how much yarn you will need for a project.

Plying Shells

First spin a thick and thin single yarn (see pages 132–133). The thick points of your yarn will become the shells in this example.

1 Choose a plying thread that doesn't break easily, and tie it in a knot with your handspun single. Put the knot through the leader thread loop in the orifice and start spinning in a counter-clockwise direction. As the twist travels up the ply, slide your fingers back and allow the yarn to be plied by the thread.

2 **(a)** When you ply a thin section of the yarn, keep your hands at a 70-degree angle to create a spiral effect.

+ It helps to put plenty of twist in your thick-and-thin single when you plan on creating this yarn. That way your shells don't end up becoming too loose and falling apart on your plying thread.

Materials
Spinning wheel | Handspun single-ply yarn | Strong plying thread

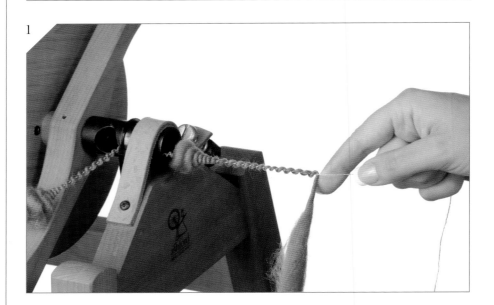

1

2a

(b) When a thick section of yarn is about to be plied, hold that yarn at a 90-degree angle and keep your fingers closer together. This will create a seashell shape in the yarn.

3 Rotate from a 90-degree angle for the thicker sections of yarn to a 70-degree angle for the thinner sections of yarn, to create seashell shapes throughout. Allow the yarn to go into the orifice before it becomes over twisted. Make sure the hooks do not catch on the yarn as it goes onto the bobbin.

Note: To secure your shells so they don't slip on your plying thread, wrap the thread around the top and base of each shell after spinning. However, if you choose not to secure your shells, you can slide them up and down the plying thread when you are weaving, knitting, or crocheting this yarn. That way your shells won't get hidden on the inside/underside of your finished item.

Note: Shellspun yarns can be worn as they are as a necklace (see Michelle Snowdon interview, pages 118–119).

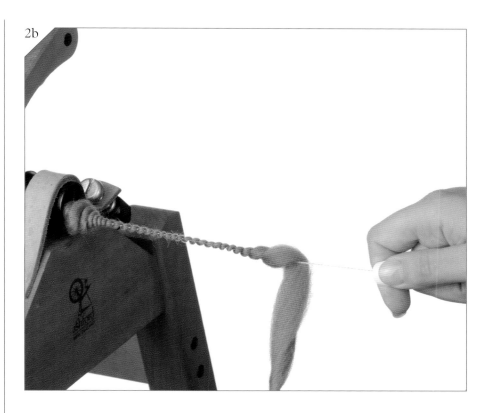

2b

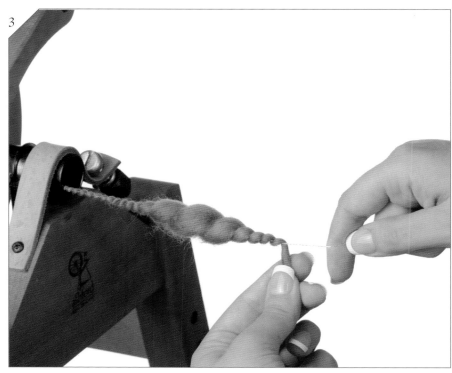

3

Plying Cocoons

Cocoons are fun textural pieces you can add into your yarn to create unique embellishments on a knit, crochet, or woven piece.

1 Choose a strong plying thread and tie it into a knot with your handspun single. Put the knot through the leader thread loop in your orifice and start spinning in a counterclockwise direction. As the twist travels up the ply, slide your fingers back and allow the yarn to be plied by the thread.

2 Begin plying the thread at a 45-degree angle. When you want to make a cocoon, hold the yarn at a 90-degree angle and begin stacking the yarn on top of itself, going backward and forward.

3 When you're done creating the cocoon, return the yarn to a 45-degree angle with the plying thread. You can make many different shapes and sizes of cocoons.

Materials
Spinning wheel | Handspun single-ply yarn | Strong plying thread

1

2

3

Navajo Plying

Navajo plying is also called chain plying. It is an easy way to turn a single yarn into a three-ply yarn. This technique is fun with thick and thin yarns as well as traditional yarns.

1 First, create a large slip-knot loop with the handspun yarn. Take this loop and put it through the loop of the leader thread in the orifice. Now take the ends of the yarn and begin treadling counterclockwise.

2 Pull a long length of yarn through the loop while you are treadling. This long length will become your next loop as the twist travels up and creates a 3-ply yarn. Continue pulling long lengths of yarn through each loop while slowly treadling and watching the twist travel up, creating another loop.

3 When you are at the end of the yarn, pull the end through the last loop and tie it into a knot.

4 When you are Navajo plying, your yarn will be three times as thick as the original single. Make sure the yarn will fit through the orifice.

+

Try Navajo plying on a kick spindle—it's great because you don't have an orifice to limit the width of the yarn you want to spin. So if you want a super-thick ropelike Navajo-plied yarn, you can easily make it on a kick spindle.

Materials
Spinning wheel | Handspun single-ply yarn

1
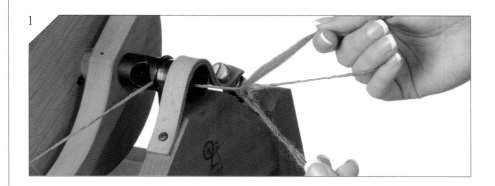

2
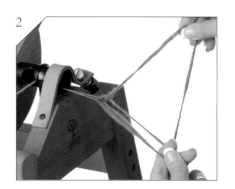

3
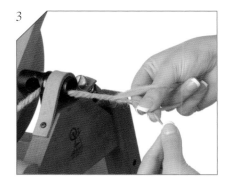

4

Art Bouclé

This technique takes two yarns and plies them together. Your single yarn must be balanced (not overspun, not underspun) for the loops to maintain their shape.

1 Choose a plying thread that does not break easily and tie in a knot with your handspun single. Put the knot through the leader loop in the orifice and start spinning in a counterclockwise direction. Hold the thread in your right hand and the yarn in your left, and begin spinning counterclockwise. Keep your hands close together, with more tension on the thread than on the yarn.

2 Using your left index finger, catch the yarn and pull up a loop. Rotate your left hand counterclockwise, wrapping the thread around the base of the loop created by the handspun yarn. The thread will come from below the loop, back toward the orifice of your wheel and around the base of the loop, returning to position below the loop.

Materials

Spinning wheel | A single or corespun yarn—choose a yarn with balance, as an overspun yarn will create twists instead of loops | A strong, thin binding thread with texture (laceweight wool or weaving threads work well)

1

2

3 Pinch the base of the new loop with your right thumb and index finger to control the twist, and allow the twist to build up.

4 Hold this pinch until you create the next loop, moving the pinch point as each new loop is formed. The twist will concentrate at the base of each loop to tighten and secure it, then balance in the space between the loops when the yarn is finished.

5 Wrapping the thread around the base of the loops will keep them from sliding down the yarn. Yarn between the loops will be plied. Compare the "plain" art bouclé (below left) with the example plied with thread (above).

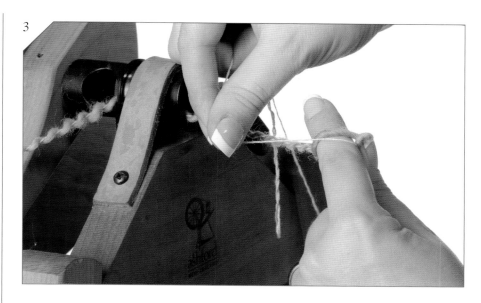

3

4

5

+ Try plying two bouclé yarns together to create the kind of yarn shown in the photo above.

+ Bouclé yarn can be spun on most wheels—however, the size of your loops may be limited by the orifice size, and the hooks on some flyers may snag loops as they are being wound on the bobbin. Loops can be as large or small as you want them to be, and are particularly dramatic when corespun yarn is used for the loops. To show off the loops in your finished projects, knit, crochet, or weave loosely so the loops have room to pop out and create the wonderful, loopy bouclé texture you were spinning for!

Sluggy Plying

This style of yarn is great for embellishments on hats or other knit or crochet garments. You can also wear this yarn just as it is, as a cowl or necklace.

1 Spin a thick and thin single while holding a thin plying thread. Hold the thread with the fiber as you spin it, to wrap it around the fiber while you're spinning. This yarn looks best when you have a variety of thick and thin sections at random.

2 After spinning this single, ply it with another strong, thin plying thread.

Materials
Spinning wheel | Fiber for spinning (roving, top, or batts) | Fine thread | Strong plying thread

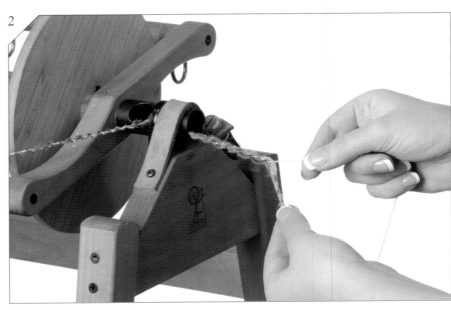

3 As you continue spinning, begin stacking the yarn in a cocoon. Make sure that the cocoon you create can fit through the orifice.

4 After making the cocoon, wrap it from end to end with the plying thread. This will create the "sluggy" section of yarn. You can wrap the cocoon as many times as you want with thread, holding securely to the single so it doesn't untwist.

5 Continue plying the single with the thread. You can add a coil or a shell at random. Or just ply it simply. Leave at least a yard or two between "slugs" for ease of knitting, crocheting, or weaving.

3

4

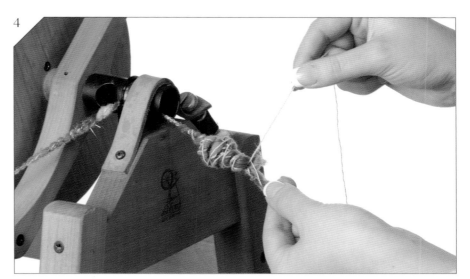

5

Recycled Yarn

You can find cones of thread at antique shops, thrift stores, yarn shops, and online. Using a strong thread as your core thread and wrapping the other threads around at a 90-degree angle will create an almost transparent yarn for knitting, weaving, or crochet.

1 Take several spools of thread or cones of yarn and place them on the floor next to your spinning wheel. To keep the threads from getting tangled, try placing them between your feet, if you are using a double treadle wheel, or on a lazy kate. Choose a strong thread to use as your core – commercial mohair works well. Experiment with various threads and yarns to create different textures and effects.

2 Tie the ends of all the yarns into a knot and place this knot into the loop of your leader thread. Begin spinning in a clockwise direction, creating a twist.

Materials
Spinning wheel | Several cones or spools of commercial thread—include at least one mohair thread | One strong core thread or handspun single-ply yarn

1

2

3 Hold your core yarn toward you and wrap all the other yarns and threads around it at a 90-degree angle. This method is just like corespinning, but using threads and yarns instead of fiber.

4 Create thick textures in the yarn by stacking the threads on top of one another, back and forth along the core, until your desired thickness is achieved.

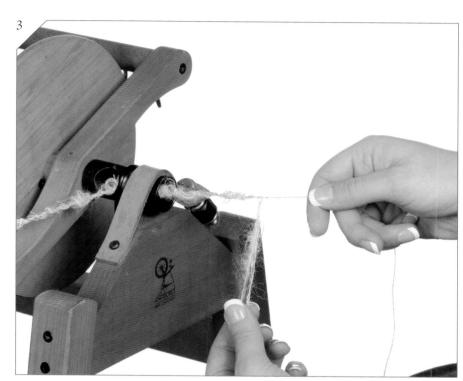

Mixed Media: Corespinning

To add smaller beads into a single-ply yarn, corespinning is a useful method. For this tutorial, freshwater pearls were used, but you can use any beads that will fit through the orifice.

1 Begin corespinning around both threads in a clockwise direction. When you are ready to add a bead, take one of the beads on the nylon thread and wrap the fiber securely before and after the bead. The more secure the fiber, the better structural integrity your yarn will have.

2 Continue corespinning and adding beads, securing them tightly with fiber, as you want them in the yarn.

Materials
Spinning wheel | Prepared fiber for spinning | Needle (make sure your needle will fit through the hole in your beads/add-ins) | Beads or other add-ins | Strong core thread | Nylon beading thread

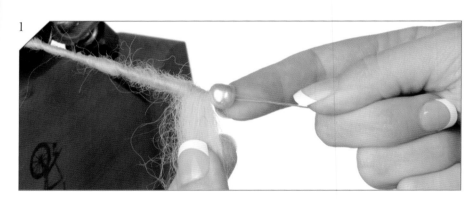
1

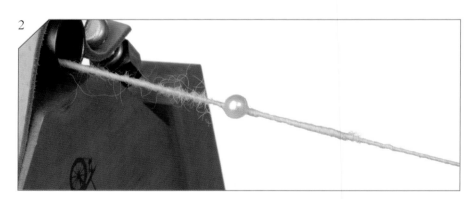
2

+ Thread the beads you want to add on strong nylon beading thread. Then tie that beading thread in a knot with the thread you will use as a core. Place both the core thread and the beading thread on your lazy kate or on opposite sides of the wheel so they do not tangle.

Mixed Media: Plying

You can add beads into your yarn while you ply. In this tutorial, beads made from seashells were used. You can add any beads to your yarn that will fit through the orifice.

1 Begin spinning in a counterclockwise direction to begin plying. Once you have plied a couple of yards, take one of the beads and bring it up to the yarn. Allow the plying thread to guide it into the yarn.

2 Don't use beads that are too heavy or bulky for this method, or they cause the finished product to sag. Small crystal or glass beads work well for this spinning method. You can also spin clusters of small beads to add sparkle and shine to your yarn without spoiling its integrity.

3 Continue plying while adding beads, making sure there is plenty of twist to secure them tightly.

+

Thread the beads you want to add onto strong plying thread. Spin a single yarn (see pages 132–133) with plenty of twist. Tie the single-ply yarn and the plying thread in a knot as you would for plying (see page 142).

Materials

Spinning wheel | Handspun single-ply yarn | Needle (make sure your needle will fit through the hole in your beads/add-ins) | Beads or other add-ins | Strong plying thread

1

2

3

Mixed Media: Single Ply

This technique can be used for feathers, strands of sequins, fabric (as shown), scraps of lace, leather, wool locks, and any other item you can imagine spinning into yarn.

1   Take a large-eyed needle and thread a tuft of wool through it. Make sure the wool has at least a 3-inch (7.5-cm) staple length for easy spinning. Insert the needle through the embellishment, leaving fiber at each end.

2   To add a bead or embellishment, start by spinning a single.

3   Take the tuft of wool and attach it to the yarn by pinching the ends of the fiber while spinning.

4   Then attach the tuft of wool back into the fiber as you continue spinning. Make sure there is plenty of twist before and after the added embellishment for structural integrity.

Materials
Spinning wheel | Fiber for spinning (any roving, top, or batt) | Large-eyed needle (make sure your needle will fit through the hole in your beads/add-ins) | Beads or other add-ins

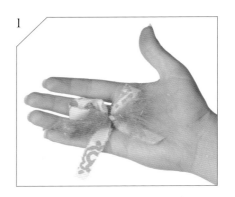

1

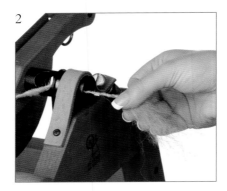

2

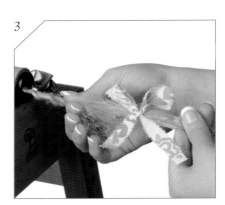

3

4

+

For beads: Thread the tuft of wool through the hole in the bead. This method will only work for beads that have somewhat large holes.

For embellishments: Thread the tuft of wool through the corner or center of the object, depending on how you want it to lay in the yarn.

Mixed Media: Fabric

Spinning yarn from fabric is a fun way to upcycle a vintage cotton pillowcase or sheet, or to transform an ugly silk blouse into a beautiful yarn.

1 Rip up your fabric into ½-inch (1.25-cm) or smaller strips. Roll the strips into a ball to keep them from tangling. Choose a strong core thread, such as hemp or weaving thread. Tie the first fabric strip and your core yarn into a knot and attach it to the leader. Begin spinning in a clockwise direction.

2 Holding the fabric at a 45-degree angle to the core thread, allow the twist to wrap the fabric around the core thread.

3 To add a new section of fabric, tuck the new end under the old end of fabric. Spin the old end over the new end for ½ inch (1.25 cm). Then bring the new end over the old end and continue spinning so that no ends are showing.

Note: You can also spin fabric with fiber. Spin a strip of fabric, then secure the end by corespinning fiber over the end. Corespin fiber for a length, then wrap the fiber over the new end of fabric and spin the fabric.

Materials
Spinning wheel | Cotton fabric torn or cut into narrow strips (vintage cotton works best) | Strong core thread (hemp or cotton thread works best)

1

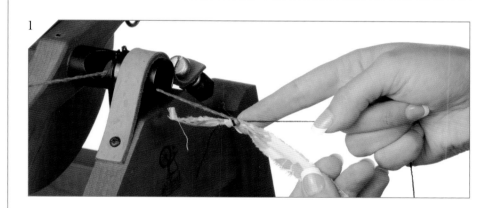

2

3

Chapter 8

Setting the Twist

This chapter covers different methods of setting yarns, as well as how to build and set yarn on a niddy noddy. It includes opinions on working with "alive" yarns, as well as traditional setting methods that have been used for generations by handspinners.

Opposite, clockwise from top left: Coiled yarn by Jessie Driscoll; yarn spun from wool locks by Robyn Story; yarn plied with thread by Ashley Martineau; yarn plied with thread by Diana North
Top: Wear your handspun yarn as an eternity scarf or cowl—yarn spun by Nicole Constantin
Bottom: Yarn plied with thread by Sayra Adams

Troubleshooting Tips

Problem: My yarn has kinks in it before setting.
Solution: Your yarn has been overspun. Setting the twist will relax many of these kinks and twists and help your yarn become balanced. Next time you spin, don't put as much twist into the fiber.

Problem: My yarn has an odor.
Solution: You can add a spoonful of white vinegar or a couple drops of lavender essential oil to the water when setting the twist.

Problem: I am concerned about moth damage.
Solution: When you soak the yarn, add a few drops of lavender essential oil or cedar oil to the water. Lavender and cedar are natural moth repellants. Store your yarn in an airtight container after it has been dried.

Problem: How do I remove grease after spinning?
Solution: Soak the yarn in soapy hot water in a sink for 15 minutes. If the water is brown, drain the water and refill the sink with fresh soapy hot water, then soak for another 15 minutes. When the soapy water no longer turns brown after adding the yarn, rinse the yarn by soaking in hot water. Hang it out to dry.

Problem: My yarn is taking a long time to dry.
Solution: Try setting the yarn in front of a fan or in the sun to speed up the drying process.

Problem: My art yarn has a fluffy/airy texture that I don't want to change or flatten by soaking it in water.
Solution: Use a steam machine (for removing wrinkles from clothes) for setting.

Problem: My traditionally spun yarn was fuzzy before it was set, and now it's flat and matted looking.
Solution: "Thwack" the yarn (like a whip) against a hard surface to fluff it up and give it that airiness. Mohair and angora-blend yarns love getting thwacked. However, don't thwack art yarns.

Setting Traditional Yarns

It's not uncommon for setting yarn to be the most popular topic at any workshop/fiber festival. Some spinners prefer the term "finish," instead of "set," as set implies that the last step in the yarn-making process somehow makes twist that doesn't want to stay, stay—and it simply doesn't do that. It's just the last, finishing, step.

The key to making good yarn is making it good on your bobbin, fixing it while you spin it, and not relying on setting, blocking, or finishing to do it for you—because it can't. A hard enough block or a hot enough steam can set any twist in any yarn but there's always a tradeoff in terms of quality. Besides giving you a false balance and an untrue set, it relieves your handspun yarn of its life, loft, and elasticity. Don't subject your wonderful work to stretching, weighting, and wet tensioning. (Steam setting is different.)

When to finish?

Just about every yarn (except for those you might use for collapse weave or energized knitting) should be finished. However, it's not terribly important how soon after spinning you do it. No matter how long your single or plied yarn has remained on its bobbin, as soon as you plunge it into water, all its twist will be activated.

Which method?

There are several ways to finish yarn, depending on the fiber. Wool yarns are typically finished in one of three ways: bathing, fulling, or steaming.

The easiest way is in a hot bath. This basic method is wonderful for yarns that have fewer than two rotations in the skein, giving it the chance to be the softest, loftiest, most elastic yarn it can be. Toss that figure-eight tied skein into a hot bath and let it soak for a bit. Once it's wet and plump, either spin it out in a salad-type spinner or wrap it in a towel and squeeze, give it a gentle "snap," then hang it, unweighted/unstretched, to dry. This is easy, low impact, and unstressful. It doesn't change your yarn in any long-lasting way except to allow the fibers to bloom a bit (which can really change your knitting gauge, so finish before you swatch).

Top: Coiled yarn by Jessie Driscoll
Bottom: Yarn plied with thread by Ashley Martineau
Opposite: Two-ply yarn by Robyn Story

If you have a singles yarn or a yarn is not perfectly balanced, consider the fulling method. Make sure you tie the skein in lots of places. The more you plan on fulling, the more figure-eights you should tie. Here are the basic elements: temperature change, agitation, and soap—the more you increase any of those elements, the more extreme results you get. Moving your yarn from a hot sink to a cold sink several times should provide temperature change enough to give you just a bit of fulling. If you want more, how about a thwack? Follow the guidelines for basic bathing above until you get to the gentle snap part, then give it a thwack instead! The more you thwack, the fuller your yarn will be. For a more extreme fulling effect, combine high temperatures, agitation, and soap by putting the yarn in a washing machine with detergent. Check it often and in no time at all you'll have a completely fulled yarn. Keep in mind that as you full your yarn you will relieve it of loft, elasticity, and length.

A very effective way of finishing yarn is to steam it. This method works well for yarns that have more twist than you want them to have. In other words, it's great for taming a wayward yarn. Hold your yarn under a bit of tension so that it hangs straight, and put it in the pathway of steam, being careful not to burn yourself. You can use a pot of boiling water, a hot teapot, or a home clothing/drapery steamer. Unlike a basic finish, a steam finish will actually change the make-up of yarn. The steaming process causes individual polypeptide chains to burst, shift against each other, find their equilibrium, and form new chains in this more stable position. If you're already happy with your yarn, steaming won't give you anything that a basic finishing bath can't provide, and will most often result in a less elastic and less lofty yarn. Steaming yarn is a bit of a correcting finish.

Text by Jacey Boggs

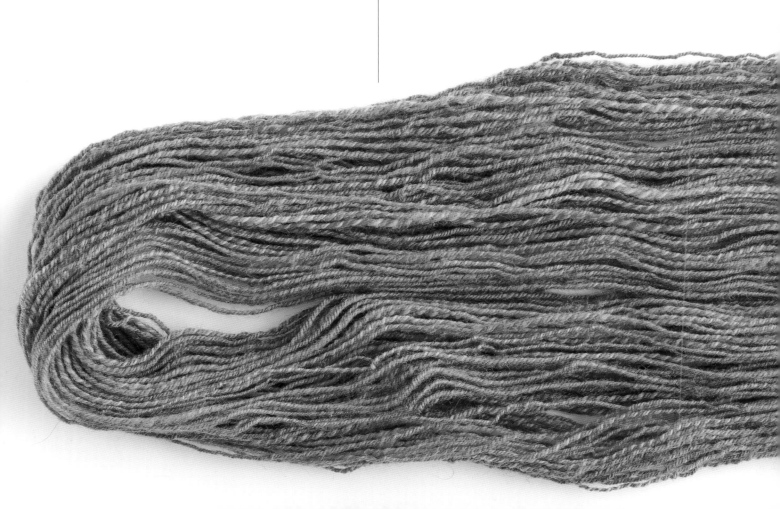

Setting Art Yarns

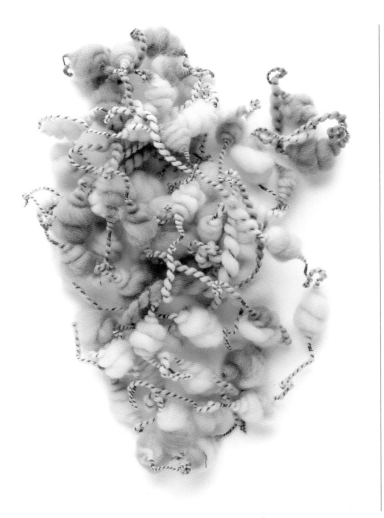

You can set art yarns on your niddy noddy. Instead of soaking the yarn in water, use a steamer to set the yarn. This is great for yarns with lots of texture and elements you don't want to squish or pull, or fibers that might flatten if saturated.

Wind your yarn onto the niddy noddy and use the appropriate setting on your steamer to set the yarn. Then remove the yarn from the niddy noddy and hang until completely dry.

Some art yarns don't need to be set, and there is no rule saying you have to set every yarn you work with. Whether or not you need to set the yarn depends on what you are planning on making with it. Yarn for socks and sweaters always needs to be set, but yarn for art projects and free-form crochet may not require setting.

Top left: Bubbly-ply yarn by Ashley Martineau
Bottom left: Coiled yarn from wool locks by Jessie Driscoll
Opposite: Bubbly-ply yarn by Ashley Martineau

Building a Niddy Noddy

A niddy noddy is used to make skeins from yarn before you wash it. A plastic niddy noddy is essential for setting yarns because you can soak the niddy noddy in water without damage, and even set it outside in the sun to dry without damaging it. Here, a 2-yard (1.8-m) niddy noddy is shown.

1 Take the 6-in (15-cm) long pieces of PVC pipe, and stick them into the T-joint. Take the 16-in (40-cm) length of PVC pipe, and connect the two T-joints together.

2 Then turn one of the T-joints 90 degrees, so that it is perpendicular to the T-joint opposite.

Materials
4 × 6-in (15-cm) long pieces of ½ in (1.25 cm) PVC pipe | 1 16-in (40-cm) long piece of ½ in (1.25 cm) PVC pipe | 2 ½ in (6.25 cm) PVC T-joints

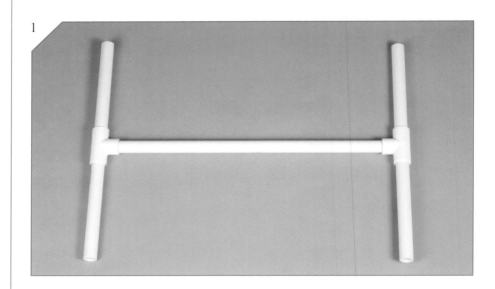

1

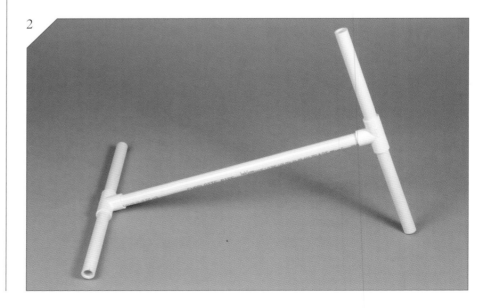

2

+
Make a 1-yard (90-cm) niddy noddy by cutting the 16-inch (40-cm) length of PVC pipe in half (8 inches/20 cm) for wrapping smaller skeins of yarn. Bulkier yarns require a 2-yard niddy noddy, but fine-weight yarns can be set on a 1-yard niddy noddy.

Using a Niddy Noddy

1 Take the end of your yarn and tie it to one of the T bars of the niddy noddy.

2 Wrap the yarn down around the other T and back up, creating a V.

3 Continue creating a V by looping the yarn back down and up, down and up. Your niddy noddy will have two V's of yarn facing each other.

4 Tie the yarn together in four places to keep it from tangling.

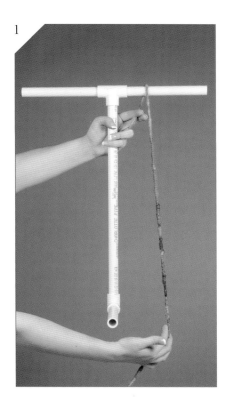

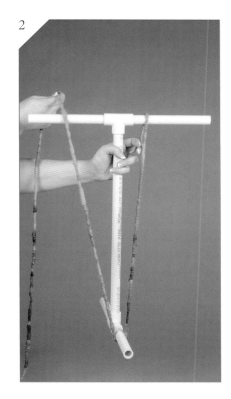

Alive Yarns

Many spinners have discovered the challenges and thrills of working with yarns that have not been set. These yarns are also known as "energized yarns," and they tend to have more dimension and personality than traditionally set yarns. This is a matter of preference and is worth a try.

In order to knit, crochet, or weave with alive yarns, simply keep the yarns on your bobbin and work off there. You can also wind the yarn into a ball if you have a limited number of bobbins for your wheel.

Many fiber artists enjoy the spontaneity of working with alive yarns. The distinctive texture, twist, and energy within the yarn creates a unique, unpredictable shape that works well for hats, scarves, mittens, and winter accessories.

Keep in mind that anything you create from alive yarn will change shape and lose its dimensionality if you block it flat. So if you want your finished piece to maintain the preset look, do not block or saturate it in water. Instead, spot clean and air dry it.

Top left: Alive yarn spun by Stephanie "Wildwoman" Fisher
Bottom left: Fabric yarn spun by Khristina Thayer
Opposite: Many spinners enjoy knitting and crocheting with yarns before they have been set

Gallery

Handspun Yarns

Opposite: Yarn by Amber Churchill of Designs by Amber
Top left: Two-ply yarn by Nicole Constantin of Rose Nectar Couture
Bottom left: Yarn by Diana North
Right: Yarn by Steph Gorin of LOOP

Opposite: Yarn by Gigi Yamashita
Above: Yarn with buttons by Nicole Constantin of Rose Nectar Fiber Couture

Top: Yarn by Michelle Snowdon of Wooldancer
Bottom: Yarn by Nicole Constantin of Rose Nectar Fiber Couture
Opposite: Yarn by Jenny Neutron Star of Takara Town

Ruru Mori

Ruru Mori has always been fascinated by yarns in extraordinary colors and textures, so she was excited and surprised to discover that there were many spinners around the world who share her passion. Ruru is always looking for new techniques and tools to create her unique art yarns.

Ruru's passion is to create yarn that reflects the beauty of nature, feelings, and objects around her. "First I select a fiber, color, and technique—then with my imagination I begin to spin. I also enjoy the accidental encounters and discoveries that I make while spinning the yarn."

Ruru uses spinning as a way to describe and remember the changes that happen in nature around her home, the scenes and memories of her travels around the world, the art museums she has visited, and ancient treasures she sees at flea markets and antique stores. Each of Ruru's yarns is a time capsule for her memories, feelings, and inspirations. "Every scene of my past experiences is the fountain of my inspiration."

"First I select a fiber, color, and technique then with my imagination I begin to spin."

To enable her to turn her inspiration into an artwork any time, Ruru dyes her fibers in many and various colors and tones. "I may need several tones of green to blend to express a specific green from my inspiration. I also use different fibers, depending on what I am spinning. I enjoy using my own hand-dyed locks and carding my own batts."

"My favorite technique is a twist with something. For example, I set glass beads at the end of a twist or pompom. Another favorite technique is corespinning coils. This technique creates a dimensional yarn that I can't wait to see when it is completed."

Ruru's favorite fibers are kid mohair and Gotland. She uses kid mohair for most of her yarn. "Adding kid mohair gives softness and dimension. I love the elegant gloss of Gotland. I love long and curly wools and fibers. I also like Wensleydale or Teeswater, but those are difficult to find in Japan. I would use those fibers all the time if they were available in Japan."

Ruru's hope is that her yarns will bring a piece of happiness to people's lives.

"Every scene of my past experiences is the fountain of my inspiration."

Opposite: Yarn spun with dragonflies made from fused Angelina and beads by Ruru Mori
Above: Yarn spun with puffs of wool by Ruru Mori

Spinning Jenny
Thread Wrap Silk

yarn

with a spin

HANDSPUN YARN, BULKY
THREAD WRAPT COILED
WOOL & SILK

www.yarnwithaspin.co.uk

Section Four
Going Professional

Chapter 9

Developing a Brand

Inspired to make a little money from your newfound love of spinning yarn?
This chapter will cover everything from selling at local farmers' markets and
craft stores to opening an online store and selling your yarns there. It discusses
photography, building a lightbox for taking great photos, being a vendor at major
fiber events, and discovering your creative niche in the spinning market.

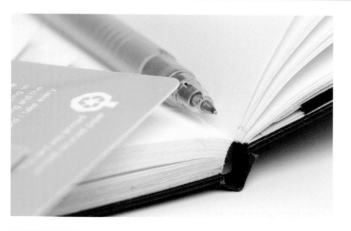

Opposite, clockwise from top left: Handspun yarn by Renae Scartabello; use handspun yarn to attach your tags to your wares; business cards from artisan shops around the world
Top: Wool cowl knit from handspun yarn by Amy Higgins Stambaugh
Bottom: Keep notes about your customers. Remembering small details is often much appreciated

Troubleshooting Tips

Problem: There aren't any yarn stores or markets in my town where I can sell my yarns or fibers in person.
Solution: Try contacting yarn stores within your state/country to see if they'd be interested in selling your yarns. Often yarn stores will have a website with an email address. You can always ship your yarns to yarn stores if you can't get there. Also, consider opening an online shop where you can advertise and sell your yarns or fibers to customers worldwide.

Problem: I spent all day at a farmers' market/craft show and I didn't sell anything. What did I do wrong?
Solution: There are multiple factors that count toward having a successful show at a market or fair. Did you have clear prices on everything? Did you have a range of items in multiple price brackets for people to choose from? How many people were at the event? Talk to the other vendors to see how they did. Was it a slow day all around? Were you the only fiber artisan selling there? If so, try selling your wares at a yarn- or fiber-specific event.

Problem: I have an online shop and I haven't sold anything in months.
Solution: How much time are you putting into your online shop? If you listed a handful of items months ago and expected sales to follow, it's possible your shop has gone stale while you were waiting. Artisans who run successful shops never wait for things to sell; they are always busy adding more inventory. Try taking new photos of your items. A clean white background will make your yarns or fibers shine. Review your pricing—look at other yarn and fiber shops online and see what their price range is. Also, compare your shipping costs to other online shops. Inflated shipping prices will often turn buyers away. Ideally you should be adding new products to your shop every week. The more products you have in store, the more likely something is to sell. Consider running a special coupon or offer, or offering free shipping for a month.

Inspiration

Fiber art has probably been around for over 10,000 years. The very first articles of woven fabric that we know of (about 3,000 years old) were handcrafted with levels of skill far beyond what our commercial mills are doing today. There is no way to research where ancient artisans got their ideas from. But none of us are complete originals—we are all standing on the shoulders of those before us.

On the opposite page are three yarns: one spun by the author, one spun by Heather Lightbody, and one spun by Lisa Renee McKenzie. The author asked the others to spin a yarn inspired by the yarn she had spun. "Copy me, but make it your own," she said, knowing their strong artistic voices would show through in their yarns.

Observe the end result and how each yarn is different and yet similar. The similarities you will find from skein to skein have to do with the spinning techniques—all of which no spinner can claim as their own.

However, the differences are in the textures, the wools, the dyes, the colors, the threads, and the artistic elements. This is where creativity happens. Focus on these elements in your yarns to create an original product.

If your idea is almost exactly like someone else's, try adding or changing three elements of it to differentiate yourself and create a truly unique product.

Top: This skein of yarn was spun from natural wool top and plied with novelty bouclé nylon thread and curly dyed wool locks
Opposite: Top yarn spun by Ashley Martineau; middle yarn spun by Lisa Renee McKenzie; bottom yarn spun by Heather Lightbody

Photography

Many spinners struggle with taking professional-quality photos. Your goal as a photographer is to take pictures that could be framed on a wall as art. Each picture should capture the texture, color, and personality of the fiber in an aesthetically pleasing way.

Photography is one of the most challenging aspects of running an online business, and many online shops struggle and fail solely because of bad photographs. So take a moment, look at other shops, write down what you admire about the photography, and practice, practice, practice.

Here are some simple tips you can follow to improve the quality of your photos and make your yarns and fibers more appealing to buyers.

Never use flash

Always take your photos in bright, clean, natural light from a window or in a well-lit lightbox (see page 186). Using a flash makes yarns and fibers look dingy, dirty, and old.

Pay attention to white balance

Do you have problems with your photos looking blue or yellow? This is because your camera doesn't understand the color white and is trying to fix it for you. For indoor photos (like in your lightbox) change the white balance to "tungsten." This will remove that dingy yellow look from your photos. For outdoor photos change the white balance to "sunny" or "cloudy." This will keep your photos from turning blue. Many newer cameras have a white balance called "auto" that works in all environments.

Use the macro setting

This button looks like a tiny tulip flower on most cameras, and it is used for taking close-up shots to help the camera focus on the detail of the image. It basically makes your camera near-sighted, so that you can capture every lock and curl of fiber. Always have your camera set on macro when taking pictures of yarn.

Think about presentation

Do your yarns look fat, alive, and happy in photographs? Or do they look deflated, limp, and lifeless? Look at other photographs spinners have taken on Etsy, and see how they display their wares. A popular way of displaying fiber is in a circle, either braided or loose. This way the customer can see the color changes in the dyelot. Yarns can be photographed as skeins or as twisted piles. Batts can be difficult to photograph, and can be rolled up, unrolled, half-rolled, or ripped in half and rolled on top of each other at right angles.

Opposite: Yarn by Lisa Renee McKenzie

Building a Lightbox

Clean, professional-looking photos are a must-have when opening and running an online shop. Here is an easy and affordable way of building a mini studio in which to photograph your yarns and fibers.

1 Clamp the spotlights onto the top and sides of the plastic bin. Take the craft foam or poster board and position it inside the bin so that the back and base of the bin is covered in white. Cut it to fit if you need to.

2 Turn on the lamps and adjust the lighting to fill in any gray areas. Place your yarn in the center and adjust the lamps as necessary. Try having one lamp shining behind the yarn to prevent shadow, and two lamps shining at angles in front of the yarn.

3 When you are done taking pictures of your yarns and fibers, simply place all your supplies inside the plastic bin and cover it and store it until the next time you are ready to take photographs.

Materials
3 clip-on office spotlights | Clear plastic storage bin | White craft foam or posterboard

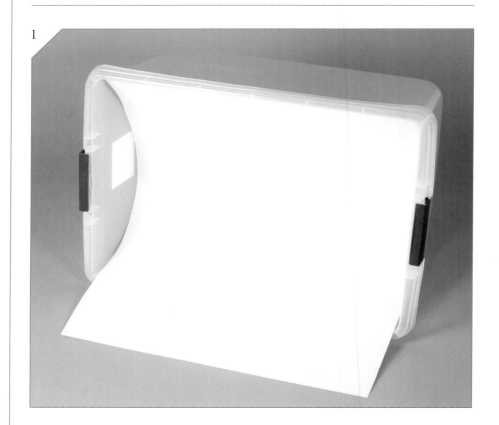

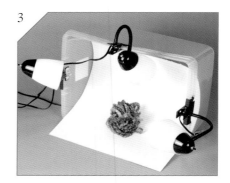

Opposite: A lightbox is a great way to photograph yarns, but many yarns look best when photographed in a natural setting. This also gives your online customers a true idea of the yarn's thickness, texture, and length. Make sure the props you use to display your yarn don't detract from the photo.
Yarn by Lisa Renee McKenzie

Vending Tips

First, find out what's going on in your area. Search online for local yarn stores, craft fairs, art fairs, farmers' markets, and fiber and yarn events.

Yarn stores are a great way to sell your yarns and fibers without the time commitment of vending at a show. Search for local yarn stores online, and email or phone them to set up an appointment. Then take a basket of your yarns to each one to see if they think their customers would be interested. Some stores may want traditional handspun yarn; others may want art handspun. Some shops will purchase your yarns wholesale, and some may want you to sell on consignment.

Fiber and yarn events have a great potential for profit because there are lots of people there shopping specifically for fiber-related items. However, you will have to work hard to stand out and attract customers to your booth. Often customers save up and are looking for deals and special items that will make their trip memorable. The costs of attending these shows can add up quickly (booth rental fee, gas, food) so make sure your inventory will cover all your expenses.

More general craft festivals, art fairs, and farmers' markets can be hit and miss. Before you commit to being a vendor at one of these events, go along as a visitor and see what other vendors are selling. Will you be one of many fiber artists, or will you be the only one there in your niche? Look at the price points of other vendors at the festival. Selling expensive boutique items at a free farmers' market is a waste of your time. It is important to have a wide variety of items for this kind of event. Finished knit or crochet items tend to sell better at these events than yarn and fiber. Talk to other vendors at these shows and ask about their experiences of being a vendor there.

Text by Esther Rodgers

Left: Business cards from fiber artists around the world
Opposite: Make sure your business cards match your yarn labels and website. All of your marketing materials should match your brand

Festival checklist

- Booth: tent, folding chairs, tables and tablecloths, sign/banner, plastic painters, drop cloths to close off booth at night, handtruck.
- Display: racks, fixtures, grid walls, baskets, dress forms, mannequins, heads, samples.
- Marketing: mailing list, business cards, flyers, notecards for quickie signs.
- Miscellaneous: clipboard, lights, cords and extension cords, surge protectors, trash bags, mirror (if you have any wearables).
- Tools: screwdrivers, box cutter, pocket knife, wrench, pliers, clothes pins, duct tape, paper clips, hammer, zipties, scissors, hole punch.
- Food: cooler with water, snacks.
- Transactions: money box, receipt books, pens, price tags, credit card machine, phone charger, bags.

Selling Online

There are many options for selling your yarns and fibers online, but a great starting point for beginning fiber artists is Etsy. The fees are low, the traffic is high, and they have a free online Seller Handbook full of advice and articles to help you get started and maintain a successful shop.

One of the keys to selling online is excellent photography. Many of the most successful sellers use crisp, white backgrounds that look clean and professional (see pages 184–187 for more on photography). Clear and concise descriptions are also necessary to market your handcrafts to buyers. Linking your online shop with social networking sites such as Facebook and Twitter will help to increase traffic.

Blogging

If you have the time, you can blog about your business—post tutorials and videos of projects you're working on, video blogs of local yarn shops and fiber festivals that you visit, and offer behind-the-scenes tours of your studio. Customers like to feel a personal connection to the artisans they are purchasing from.

Pricing

To make sure your items are priced fairly, visit other shops on Etsy and see how much they sell their yarns and fibers for. Just because a fiber or yarn is listed at a high price, doesn't mean it will sell, though. "Sold" listings will give you the best idea of what customers are actually purchasing.

Marketing

In each of your shipped packages, include a handwritten thank-you note and your business card. You can use your business cards as product tags. You can also include a small skein of sample yarn or a mini batt for customers to play with. Remember to add care instructions for items that have been knitted or crocheted from yarn. Your goal as a seller is to be remembered by your customers and give them a good reason to come back to your shop.

Networking

Create a Facebook page for your shop/business and invite your friends to become fans. Join the "Fiber Artists Marketplace" and "Fiber Artists and Yarn Spinners" groups on Facebook to learn from other sellers and market your products. Join Ravelry and create a group for your shop/business to post your sales and new inventory. There are also groups on Ravelry where you can market your products.

Never be afraid to ask questions. Some sellers may not want to talk about what makes their business successful, but most are more than willing to share their experiences.

Opposite: Your online shop should have a clean, professional appearance. Adding new products every week will keep your shop looking fresh and will help increase sales

Shipping and Handling

Poly mailer bags are perfect for shipping yarns and fibers around the world. Many online shops network with PayPal to receive and process payment. You can easily transfer your money from Paypal to your bank account in a couple of clicks.

Once you sell a yarn or fiber in your online shop, you can log in to your PayPal account and click on "Create Shipping Label." Follow the simple directions to print your label, tape it well to your package, and schedule a pickup or dropoff at the post office.

You can take this opportunity to include some goodies and gifts in your package for your customer. This will help your customer feel appreciated and make your shop more memorable. Here are some tips from other fiber artists on what they include in their packages:

I include a free sample of spinning fiber if they ordered spinning supplies. And I often include a discount code for their next purchase and always a personal note of thanks. **Renée Williamson Jones**

I often find myself reordering more often from those who include swag than those who don't. It is a personal touch that is much appreciated by my customers and there have even been a few that wrote me to let me know that. **Melissa Bohrtz**

I wrap my goodies for customers in tissue paper and then tie like a present. Someone did this for me and I will always remember that; it made my purchase that much more special. **Kelly Keson Miller**

I want people to feel like they are receiving a gift—as I try to put great care in making things to sell. Plus, this is not a necessity item, and could be a purchase from someone trying to treat themselves to something fun and special to them. I want the person who purchased to be delighted. **Kristine Haddock**

Fiber comes with dried lavender and a fiber sample if it is available. All tied with a ribbon, with business cards and a personal note of thanks. It is work, but I thought a long time about it and this is how I would want my fiber to arrive to me. It is a gift of my time to show my appreciation to each customer for their order. **Ruth Pohl Hawkins**

I love getting cute little extras with my orders. It makes me feel all warm and fuzzy inside … **Leilani Alexander**

Left: Yarn ready to ship, spun by Adele Michelson
Opposite: Yarn by Ashley Martineau

HANDSPUN YARN, BULKY
THREAD WRAPT COILED
WOOL & SILK

with a spin

Resources

Useful Websites

Continuing Education
www.artofspinning.com
www.facebook.com/groups/fiberartists
joyofhandspinning.com
www.ravelry.com
www.youtube.com
www.youtube.com/neauveaufiberarts

Fiber Processing Equipment & Supplies
www.bluemountainhandcrafts.com
www.coppermoose.com
www.craigslist.org
www.facebook.com/groups/rawwoolforsale
www.kbbspin.org
www.ravelry.com/groups/spinners-marketplace

Dyes
www.dharmatrading.com
www.jacquardproducts.com
www.prochemicalanddye.com

Fiber Wholesalers
www.ashlandbay.com
www.embellishmentvillage.com
www.louet.com
www.paradisefibers.com
www.rhlindsaywool.com
www.thesheepshedstudio.com
www.thewoolery.com
www.worldofwool.co.uk

Online Storefronts
www.artfire.com
www.bigcartel.com
www.etsy.com
www.storenvy.com

Marketing Materials
www.moo.com
www.vistaprint.com

Social Networking & Marketing
www.craftgawker.com
www.craftsy.com
www.facebook.com
www.facebook.com/groups/fiberartistsmarketplace
www.handmadeology.com
www.pinterest.com
www.twitter.com

Blogging
www.blogger.com
www.wordpress.com

Previous pages: Yarn by Nicole Constantin
Opposite: A collection of handspun yarns from
artisans around the world

Further Reading

Color in Spinning
Deb Menz
(Interweave, 2005)

Fleece and Fiber Sourcebook
Deborah Robson and Carol Ekarius
(Storey, 2011)

Get Spun
Symeon North
(Interweave, 2010)

Hand Spun
Lexi Boeger
(Quarry Books, 2012)

Harvesting Color
Rebecca Burgess
(Artisan, 2011)

The Intentional Spinner
Judith MacKenzie McCuin
(Interweave, 2008)

In Sheep's Clothing
Nola and Jane Fournier
(Interweave, 2003)

Intertwined
Lexi Boeger
(Quarry Books, 2010)

Respect the Spindle
Abby Franquemont
(Interweave, 2009)

Sit and Spin
Jacey Boggs
(DVD)

Spin Art
Jacey Boggs
(Interweave, 2012)

Spin Artiste
Arlene Ciroula
(www.spinartiste.com)

Spin Control
Amy King
(Interweave, 2009)

Spinning in the Old Way
Priscilla A. Gibson-Roberts
(Nomad Press, 2006)

Glossary

Balanced yarn A plied yarn that doesn't twist on itself.

Batt Fiber that has been carded from hand cards or a drum carder.

Blend Two or more types of fibers combined and carded together.

Bobbin A spool that the yarn is wound onto as it is spun.

Carding This is the process of opening and preparing fibers for spinning or felting. It can refer to hand cards, drum carders, or mechanically carded fibers.

Cellulose fiber A fiber made from plants, such as hemp, cotton, or ramie.

Citric acid An acid used for setting dyes on protein-type fibers such as wool.

Coated fleeces Fleeces from sheep that have been covered with special coats to keep the wool clean and free of vegetable matter.

Colored wool Wool from naturally nonwhite fleeces.

Combing A fiber preparation technique that aligns all of the fibers in a parallel fashion.

Crimp The tiny waves found in locks of wool.

Diz A piece of equipment used to form combed fibers into an even and consistent top for spinning. The size of the hole determines the size of the top.

Doff To remove fibers from hand cards or a drum carder.

Domestic wool Wool that has been produced in your own country.

Double drive A type of wheel where the flyer and bobbin both have drive belts that are driven by the drive wheel.

Drafting The process of pulling on the fibers and feeding them from the drafting hand to the spinning hand. The drafting hand manages the fiber thickness and the spinning hand manages the twist.

Drive band A cord that goes around the spinning wheel. These come in different sizes.

Drum carder This piece of equipment makes a batt of fiber that can be spun.

Dye Any substance that is used to apply color to fibers.

Fiber Anything that can be spun into a thread or yarn.

Fleece The wool from one sheep is a fleece.

Flyer A U-shaped piece of wood with hooks lined up on one or both arms.

Footman The bar that connects the treadle to the fly wheel and causes it to turn.

Gradient dyeing The technique of dyeing fibers so that the color runs from dark through light.

Guard hair Hairs in a fleece that are coarse and stiff.

Hackle looks like a comb but is used to blend fibers. These are usually longer pieces that are mounted onto a work surface.

Handspun Yarns spun by hand on a spinning wheel or spindle.

Immersion dyeing the technique of dyeing fibers by immersing them in a dye solution.

Lamb's wool The first shearing from the sheep, usually before it is one year old.

Lanolin The greasy, sticky coating that is on wool before it has been washed.

Lazy kate The upright posts that hold the flyer and the bobbin.

Leader A length of yarn that is attached to the bobbin— it is used as a starter yarn to spin new yarn by joining it onto the leader.

Lock A small, approximately finger-sized bit of wool that tends to stay together when shorn from the sheep.

Loft The airiness of the fleece, yarn, or roving. Fluffy and airy is good, as it increases warmth and makes the yarn soft to the touch.

Luster The shiny appearance of wool, particularly longer stapled wool. They really shine when spun as a worsted yarn.

Neps Small nubs of fiber that are usually removed during the spinning process.

Niddy noddy A tool used to make skeins from yarn.

Orifice The part of the spinning wheel where the leader yarn is threaded through and spun—the hole on the side of the flyer.

Raw wool Wool that has not been washed.

Rolag A cylinder-shaped roll of wool that is used to spin woolen-type yarns.

Roving A long strand of carded fiber that is a rope of ready-to-spin fiber.

Shearing The process of removing the wool from fiber animals.

Single One individual strand of spun yarn.

Skirting The removal of the waste wool from a fleece.

Solar dyeing The process of dyeing fiber by sealing it in jars with liquid dyes and heating with sunlight.

Staple length The length of a lock of wool from a fleece.

Tie dyeing The process of tying knots in fiber to form patterns on the dyed fiber.

Treadles The pedals that operate a spinning wheel.

Urea A chemical commonly added in the dyeing process, it attracts moisture and is useful for keeping the fiber damp while it absorbs the dye.

Whorl The disc that forms the base of a drop spindle.

Right: Yarn by Brittany Wilson

Contributors

A special thanks to each and every one who contributed to this book. I couldn't have done it without you!

Arlene Ciroula of Spin Artiste
www.spinartiste.com

Beth of Blue Mountain Handcrafts
www.bluemountainhandcrafts.com

Esther Rogers of Jazz Turtle Creations
www.jazzturtle.etsy.com

Heather Lightbody of Girl with a Hook
www.girlwithahook.com

Jacey Boggs of Insubordiknit
www.insubordiknit.com

Lexi Boeger of Pluckyfluff
www.pluckyfluff.com

Melissa Yoder Ricks of Wild Hare Fiber Studio
www.wildharefiber.com

Michelle Snowdon of Wool Dancer
www.wooldancer.com

Ruru Mori of Happy Spinning
www.happyspinning.com

Sayra Adams of Atomic Blue
www.atomicbluefiber.com

Tina Watson of Herman Hills Knittery
www.hermanhillsknittery.com

Fiber contributors
Adele Michelson of Loolie Mom Fiber Arts
www.looliemom.etsy.com

Alliston Findlay of AF Handcrafts
www.AFhandcrafts.etsy.com

Amber Churchill of Designs by Amber
www.designsbyamber.etsy.com

Brittany Wilson of Boho Knitter Chic Spins
www.bohoknitterchic.etsy.com

Christina MacDowell of Twisted and Treadled
www.etsy.com/shop/TwistedandTreadled

Elizabeth Conway of Fibers 4 Ewe
www.fibers4ewe.net

Elizabeth Stottlemeyer of Hobbledehoy
www.hobbledehoy.etsy.com

Elysa Darling of 222 Handspun
www.222handspun.com

Gigi Yamashita
http://hataori.jugem.jp

Jackie Ottino Graff of Dye Mama Wool Works
www.dyemama.etsy.com

Jennifer Gallentine of Willow Mist Acres
www.willowmistacres.etsy.com

Jess of Knotty Ewe
www.shetibo.etsy.com

Karla V Muntane of Spinning Mermaid
www.spinningmermaid.com

Kate Heffer of Knits and 'Nacks
www.knitsandnacks.etsy.com

Kathryn Narach O'Donovan of Dragonfly Fiber Art
www.dragonflyfiberart.etsy.com

Kelly Argue of Felting Sunshine
www.FeltingSunshine.etsy.com

Kestrel McCarthy of Corn Creek Fiber
www.corncreekfiber.etsy.com

Kimberly Buchy of Woodland Hills Alpacas
www.woodlandhillsalpacas.com

Lisa Check of Flying Goat Farm
www.flyinggoatfarm.etsy.com

Marcella Hogg of Hogg Wild Fibers
www.hoggwildfibers.etsy.com

Margaret Trousdale of The Yarn Marm
www.theyarnmarm.blogspot.com

Mary Egbert of Camaj
www.camaj.etsy.com

Melissa Bohrtz of Hello Purl
www.hellopurl.com

Pam Blasko of Pam's Fiber
www.pamsfiber.etsy.com

Patricia Briceño of Beesybee Fibers
www.beesybee.etsy.com

Patti Richards of Funky Yarns
www.funkyarns.etsy.com

Rachel Jones of On the Round
www.ontheround.etsy.com

Rachel Kluesner of Dyeabolical Yarns
www.dyeabolicalyarns.com

Rita Petteys of Yarn Hollow
www.yarnhollow.etsy.com

Robyn Story of Yarns and Storys
www.yarnsandstorys.etsy.com

Samantha LaRue of Punk n Sparkle
www.punknsparkle.etsy.com

Sandy Ryan of Homestead Wool and Gift Farm
www.homesteadwoolandgiftfarm.com

Sarah Hollandsworth of Yarn Geek Fibers
www.yarngeekfibers.com

Shannon Herrick of The Spun Monkey Fiber Studio
www.thespunmonkey.com

Stacy Shipley of Lush Fiber Farm
www.lushfiberfarm.com

Tal Hadini of New Twist
www.newtwist.etsy.com

Right: Yarn by Ashley Martineau

Yarn contributors

Adele Michelson of Loolie Mom Fiber Arts
www.looliemom.etsy.com

Allison Jai O'Dell of CompassioKnit
www.allisonjai.com

Amber Churchill of Designs by Amber
www.designsbyamber.etsy.com

Amy Higgins Stambaugh of Wool Crush
www.etsy.com/people/bigwoolcrush

Brittany Wilson of Boho Knitter Chic Spins
www.bohoknitterchic.etsy.com

Debbie Johnson of Hampton Artistic Yarns
www.hamptonartisticyarns.com

Debra Lambert of Picasso's Moon
www.picassosmoonyarn.com

Diana North of FeistyFenn Fibers
www.feistyfennfibers.etsy.com

Elizabeth Stottlemeyer of Hobbledehoy
www.hobbledehoy.etsy.com

Gigi Yamashita
http://hataori.jugem.jp

Jenny Neutron Star of Takara Town
www.takaratown.com

Jessie Driscoll of Stash Enhancement
www.stashenhancement.etsy.com

Khristina Thayer of The Naked Ewe
www.thenakedewe.etsy.com

Kimi Tran of NorahBe
www.norahbe.etsy.com

Kristine Haddock of Storybook Fibers
www.storybookfibers.etsy.com

Leslie Hulbert of Lollyarn
www.lollyarn.etsy.com

Lisa Renee McKenzie of Oscar and Sophia
www.oscarandsophia.etsy.com

Melissa Bohrtz of Hello Purl
www.hellopurl.com

Melissa Lauer of ArachnesWheel/Twisted Skeins
www.twistedskeins.etsy.com

Melissa Nasby of SoulFibre
www.soulfibre.etsy.com

Monica Thompson of Just Ducky
www.justduckyhandspun.com

Nicole Constantin of Rose Nectar Fibre Couture
www.rosenectar.etsy.com

Pam Blasko of Pam's Fiber
www.pamsfiber.etsy.com

Reiko Usada of Reiko Mono
www.reikomono.com

Renae Scartabello of Terra Bella Spun
www.terrabellaspun.etsy.com

Robyn Story of Yarns and Storys
www.yarnsandstorys.etsy.com

Shannon Herrick of The Spun Monkey Fiber Studio
www.thespunmonkey.etsy.com

Steph Gorin of LOOP
www.loop.etsy.com

Stephanie "Rosie" Fisher of Wildwoman Creations
www.wildwomancreations.com

Suzy Brown of Wool Wench
www.woolwench.etsy.com

Index

acid dyeing 64, 67
Adams, Sayra 56, 161, 200
AF Handcrafts 200
agitation 163
Alexander, Leilani 192
alive yarns 160, 168
alkaline environments 66
allergies 11
alpaca 11–12, 16, 19, 23, 35, 39, 48, 64
Angelina 21
angora 17–18, 23, 33, 35, 39, 42, 48, 64, 161
animal fibers 10, 22, 24, 64–65, 76
antique shops 154
antislip pads 98
ArachnesWheel 202
Argue, Kelly 200
art fairs 188
art yarns 102–3, 119–20, 150–51, 161, 164–65, 176, 188
artisans 181–82, 190
Ashford Country Spinner 122
Atomic Blue 56, 200
AURA spinning wheel 83
auto white balance setting 184

background 181, 190
bags 188, 192
ball bearings 97
bamboo 66
bank accounts 192
barber-pole effect 106
basics of plying 142–43
bathing yarns 162
batts 19, 21, 33, 35–36, 42–45, 52–57, 87, 119, 137, 176, 184, 190
beads 108–11, 156–58, 176
Beesybee Fibers 201
Blasko, Pam 201–2
blending 11, 33–34, 44–45
blocking 162
blogging 190, 196
Blue Mountain Handcrafts 200
bobbins 121–22, 128, 142, 151, 162, 168
Boeger, Lexi 82–83, 139, 197, 200
Boggs, Jacey 163, 197, 200
Boho Knitter Chic Spins 113, 200, 202
Bohrtz, Melissa 192, 201–2
booths 188
bottom whorl spindles 88, 90–91

bouclé yarns 102, 137, 150–51
brand development 180–81
breed associations 24
Briceño, Patricia 64, 201
britch wool 25
Brown, Suzy 202
bubble plying 104, 143–44
Buchy, Kimberly 53, 200
building hackles 48–49
building lightboxes 186–87
building niddy noddies 166
building spindles 90–91, 98–99
building spinning wheels 124–31
bulky yarns 88, 91, 122
Burgess, Rebecca 197
business cards 190, 192
buying raw wool 24
buying spinning wheels 121
by-passable orifice 122

Camaj 65, 201
camping stoves 64
carders/carding 32–36, 42–45, 176
care instructions 190
caring for wool 30–31
carpet wool 14
cashmere 17
CDs 91
cellulose fibers 10, 20
chain plying 149
chairs 97, 188
Check, Lisa 200
checklists 188
Cheviot breed 13
children's spinning 88
choosing spinning wheels 122–23
Churchill, Amber 53, 171, 200, 202
Ciroula, Arlene 6, 197, 200
close-up shots 184
clouds 35, 39
cloudy setting 184
coarse wool 14
cocoon plying 148
coil corespinning 176
coil plying 104, 145
cold-water dyes 66
collapse weave 162
Columbia breed 13
combs/combing 32–34, 36, 40–41, 48

commercial powder dyes 68
CompassioKnit 202
compost 25
consignment sales 188
Constantin, Nicole 6, 97, 161, 171, 173–74, 197, 202
contributors 200–201
Conway, Elizabeth 200
Coopworth breed 15
core threads 94, 102, 140, 154
corespinning 94–95, 102, 136–38, 140, 151, 159, 176
Cormo breed 12
Corn Creek Fiber 200
Corriedale breed 13
Cotswold breed 15
cotton 20, 42, 62, 66, 76, 102, 159
coupons 181
craft fairs 181, 188
Create Shipping Label 192
creativity 182
credit card machines 188
crockpots 64
curly yarns 140, 176
customer service 190, 192

Darling, Elysa 200
Debouillet breed 12
delta orifices 122, 141
descriptions 190
Designs by Amber 53, 171, 200, 202
dimensionality 168, 176
discount codes 192
display items 188
DIY Wheels Group 124
dizzing 34, 36, 48, 50–57
Dorset breed 13
double-drive wheels 122
double-treadle wheels 122
drafting 37, 87, 92–93, 96, 101, 106, 132–33
Dragonfly Fiber Art 200
Driscoll, Jessie 117, 161–62, 164, 202
drive 122, 130
drop spindles 86–97, 100
drop spun yarns 112–17
drum carding 44–45
drying racks 28–29
drying techniques 22, 30, 161
Dye Mama Wool Works 200

dye suppliers 196
Dyeabolical Yarns 80, 201
dyeing fibers 62–83

Easter egg dyes 64, 68
ecofriendly fibers 20
Egbert, Mary 63, 201
Ekarius, Carol 197
elastic threads 102
elasticity 18, 162–63
embellishments 18, 108, 120, 148, 152, 158
energized yarns 162, 168
English rabbits 18
equipment 34–35, 124, 188, 196
essential oils 161
Etsy 96, 184, 190
event targeting 181
expenses 188
eyelash yarns 102, 137

fabric spinning 159
Facebook 190, 196
fairs 181
fancy corespinning 138
fancy plying 104
farmers' markets 181, 188
farms 24–25, 58
faux fibers 11, 21, 67
fees 188, 190
FeistyFenn Fibers 202
felting 12, 18, 22–23, 27
Felting Sunshine 200
festivals 83, 162, 188, 190
Fiber Artists Marketplace 190
Fiber Artists and Yarn Spinners 190
fiber types 10–21
fiber-reactive dyeing 66
Fibers 4 Ewe 200
figure-eights 162–63
Findlay, Alliston 53, 200
fine wool 12
fingering yarns 88
finishing 162–63
Firestar 21
Fisher, Stephanie 168, 202
flash 184
flax 20
flyers 121–22, 126–28
Flying Goat Farm 200

food colorings 64, 68
footman-to-wheel connections 129–30
Fournier, Jane 197
Fournier, Nola 197
frame-building 125–26
Franquemont, Abby 197
free shipping 181
freestyle spinning 118–19
French rabbits 18
frosting dyes 64, 68
fulling 162–63
Funky Yarns 80, 201
fuzzy yarns 141, 154, 161

Gallentine, Jennifer 200
galleries 52–59, 78–81, 112–17, 170–75
gauge 162
gel frosting dyes 68
German rabbits 18
giant rabbits 18
Giant Skein 83
Gibson-Roberts, Priscilla A. 197
Girl with a Hook 200
gloves 39, 66
goat fibers 10, 17, 23
Gorin, Steph 171, 202
Gotland yarn 176
gradient dyeing 62–63, 70–71, 77
Graff, Jackie Ottino 200
guard hair 16–18, 34

222 Handspun 200
hackles 32, 34, 36, 48–51
Haddock, Kristine 97, 113, 115, 192, 202
Hadini, Tal 201
halo effect 18, 106, 154
Hampton Artistic Yarns 202
hand carding 42–43
hand painting 62–63, 72–73, 77
hand picking 38, 134, 140
handling 192
handspinning 118, 170–75
Handspun 83, 197
Handspun Revolution 83
Happy Spinning 200
hardware 124
Hawkins, Ruth Pohl 192
Heffer, Kate 79, 200
Hello Purl 201

hemp 20, 66, 102, 137, 159
Herman Hills Knittery 24, 200
Herrick, Shannon 201–2
Hobbledehoy Fibers 55, 200, 202
Hogg, Marcella 80, 200
Hogg Wild Fibers 80, 200
Hollandsworth, Sarah 80, 201
Homestead Wool and Gift Farm 201
hook orifices 122, 141
Huacaya breed 16
Hulbert, Leslie 202
hypoallergenic fibers 11, 16

Icelandic breed 14
immersion dyeing 62–63, 68–69
inspiration 182
Insubordiknit 200
Intertwined 83, 197
inventory 181, 188, 190
Irish tension/bobbin-led wheels 122

Jazz Turtle Creations 56, 200
Johnson, Debbie 202
Jones, Rachel 201
Jones, Renée Williamson 192
jumbo flyer packages 122
Just Ducky 202

Karakul breed 14
kick spindles 96–111, 149
kid mohair 176
King, Amy 197
kinks 161
Kluesner, Rachel 80, 201
Knits and 'Nacks 79, 200
Knotty Ewe 200
Kool-aid packets 64

L-hooks 121
laceweight yarns 88
Lambert, Debra 202
LaRue, Samantha 67, 201
Lauer, Melissa 202
lavender oil 161
lazy kates 141, 156
leader threads 92, 94, 100–102, 104,
    106, 110, 132
Leicester breed 15
Lightbody, Heather 182, 200

lightboxes 184, 186–87
lighting 184
Lincoln breed 15
linen 20, 66
llamas 10, 16, 23
locks 24, 68, 72, 87, 134–35, 140, 176
loft 162–63
Lollyarn 202
longwool 15, 35
Loolie Mom Fiber Arts 200, 202
LOOP 171, 202
lubrication 97
Lush Fiber Farm 201

McCarthy, Kestrel 200
McCuin, Julia Mackenzie 197
MacDowell, Christina 200
machine washing 11
McKenzie, Lisa Renee 53, 182, 184, 202
macro settings 184
mailers 192
Majakraft 83
marketing 188, 190, 196
markets 181
Martineau, Ashley 6, 63, 87, 97, 113, 115,
    161–62, 164, 182, 192, 201
medium wool 12
melting fibers 67
Menz, Deb 197
Merino fibers 11–12, 18, 23
metallic threads 106
Michelson, Adele 192, 200, 202
microwave ovens 64
mildew 22–23, 30
Miller, Kelly Keson 192
mirrors 188
mixed media 108–11, 156–59
mohair 17, 23, 42, 64, 106, 140–41, 161, 176
Mori, Ruru 176–77, 200
moths 30, 161
mulberry silk 19
multiple colors 75
multiple price brackets 181
Muntane, Karla V. 79, 200

Naked Ewe 202
Nasby, Melissa 202
natural light 184
Navajo churro breed 14
Navajo plying 149
Neauveau Fiber Arts 113, 115, 191
neps 34, 40–41
New Twist 201
new-wave handspinning movement 118
niddy noddies 160, 164, 166–67

noils 34
NorahBe 202
North, Diana 161, 171, 202
North, Symeon 197
novelty threads/yarns 102, 106, 119, 137, 141
nylon 11–12, 21, 67

O'Dell, Allison Jai 87, 202
O'Donovan, Kathryn Narach 200
odors 161
offers 181
On the Round 201
online stores see stores; websites
orifices 121–22, 132, 141, 143, 151, 157
Oscar and Sophia 53, 202
outdoor photography 184
over-dyeing 62
overspinning 161
overtwisting 87, 121
Oxford breed 13

painting fibers 44
Pam's Fiber 201–2
payment processing 192
PayPal 192
pencil roving 92
Perendale breed 13, 15
personality of yarns 102, 119, 184
Petteys, Rita 201
pH values 64
photography 184–86, 190
Picasso's Moon 202
picked wool 35
pickers 35, 39
plant fibers 10–11, 20, 62, 66, 76
plastic niddy noddies 166
Pluckyfluff Studio 83, 139, 200
plying 95, 103–4, 106, 110–11, 121,
    142–49, 157
Polwarth breed 12
poly mailer bags 192
polypeptide chains 163
posture 97
predrafting 87
preparing fibers 32–51
presentation 184
prices 181, 188, 190
primitive breeds 14
processing methods 36–37
product tags 190
professionalism 184, 186
profit 188
protein fibers 10, 76
Punk n Sparkle 201
pygora 17

rabbits 18
Rambouillet breed 12
ramie 66
ratios 121–22
Ravelry 24, 124, 190
rayon 66
receipt books 188
recycled yarns 154–55
Reiko Mono 202
rental fees 188
repeatable yarns 122
reuse 91, 154–55, 158–59
Richards, Patti 80, 201
Ricks, Melissa Yoder 200
Robson, Deborah 197
Rogers, Esther 33, 56, 188, 200
rolags 34, 42–43
Romney breed 13, 15
Rose Nectar Fibre Couture 171, 173–74, 202
roving 34, 36, 48, 50, 87, 92
Ryan, Sandy 201

salad spinners 30, 162
sales 181, 188, 190–91
samples 58, 190, 192
Saori weaving 118
Scartabello, Renae 113, 202
Scottish blackface breed 14
Scottish tension/flyer-led wheels 122
second cuts 24–25, 34
self-striping yarns 104, 138
Seller Handbook 190
selling yarns 181
semi-transparent yarns 154
setting dyes 75
setting yarns 160–69
sheep 10–16, 23–25, 58
shell plying 104, 146–47
shellspun yarns 147
shepherds 24, 58–59
Shetland breed 13
Shipley, Stacy 201
shipping costs 181, 192
shows 181, 188
Shropshire breed 13
silks 11–12, 19, 33, 42, 64, 159
silkworms 10, 19
single ply 158
single spinning 100
single yarns 104, 108–11, 121, 132–33
single-drive wheels 122
single-treadle wheels 122
skeins 119–20, 162–63, 182, 184, 190
skirting 25–26, 33–34
sluggy plying 152–53

Snowdon, Michelle 87, 118–19, 147, 174, 200, 202
soaking wool 26
soap 163
social networking 190, 196
soda ash (sodium carbonate) 66
solar dyeing 63–64, 74–75
sold listings 190
solid colors 74
SoulFibre 202
Southdown breed 13
Spin Artiste 6, 200
spin dryers 30
spindles 149
spinning 92–94, 97, 100–101, 103, 108–9, 132–38, 140, 182
Spinning Mermaid Fibres 79
spinning wheels 83, 96–97, 100, 120–21, 124–31
sport/DK yarns 88
spot cleaning 168
spotlights 186
Spun Monkey Fiber Studio 201–2
staff 87
Stambaugh, Amy Higgins 202
Star, Jenny Neutron 174, 202
Stash Enhancement 117, 202
steam machines 161–64
storage 12, 30, 161
stores 181, 184, 188, 190, 196
Story, Robyn 87, 161–62, 201–2
Storybook Fibers 113, 115, 202
Stottlemeyer, Elizabeth 33, 55, 200, 202
stovetops 64
stretching 162
striped effects 77, 104, 138
studio building 186
sunny setting 184
super-curly yarns 140
superwash yarns 11
suppliers 196
Suri alpaca 16
swatches 162
synthetic fibers 10–11, 21, 67–68, 76

tabletop kick spindles 97
tags 188, 190
Takara Town 174, 202
Targhee breed 13
teaching spinning 88, 119, 196
Teeswater breed 15, 176
temperature change 163
tension 121–22, 129, 163
tension knobs 129
TerraBellaSpun 113, 202

test drives 121
thank-you notes 190, 192
Thayer, Khristina 168, 202
thick and thin yarns 101, 104, 132–33, 144, 146, 149
thimbles 97–99
Thompson, Monica 202
thread plying 143
thread wrapping 106–7, 141
three-ply yarns 149
thrift stores 154
thwacking 161, 163
tie dyeing 62, 76–77
tools 34–35, 124, 188
top 19, 36, 40, 42, 68, 87
top whorl spindles 88, 90–91
tops of frames 126
traditional yarn setting 162–63
traditional yarns 86–87, 122, 149, 161–63, 188
traffic 190
Tran, Kimi 202
treadles 122, 130
troubleshooting tips 11, 23, 33, 63, 87, 97, 121, 161, 181
Trousdale, Margaret 201
tungsten setting 184
tussah silk 19
twist 87, 93–94, 100, 121–22, 132–33, 136, 146, 157, 160–69, 176
Twisted Skeins 202
Twisted and Treadled 200
Twitter 190, 196
two-ply basic plying 142

unique products 182
upcycling 90–91, 159
uptake 121
Usada, Reiko 202

vegetable matter 24–26, 33–35, 40
vending tips 188
vendors 181, 188
vinegar 23, 63, 67, 161

warp thread 20
warping 29
washing fibers 22–31
washing wool 22–23, 26–27
Watson, Tina 58–59, 200
wavy yarns 143
wayward yarns 163
weather forecasts 74
websites 24, 83, 124, 181, 184, 186, 188, 190–91, 196–97, 200–202
weight of spindles 88

weighting 162
Wensleydale breed 15, 176
wet tensioning 162
wheel attachments 129
white balance 184
wholesale purchases 188, 196
whorls 88
Wild Hare Fiber Studio 200
Wildwoman Creations 168, 202
Willow Mist Acres 200
Wilson, Brittany 87, 113, 199–200, 202
wire 136–37
wirespsun yarn 136
wooden drop spindles 90
Woodland Hills Alpacas 200
wool 11–15, 19, 22–27, 30–35, 37–38, 40–41, 64, 67–69, 162
Wool Crush 202
Wool Wench 202
WoolDancer 174, 200
worsted yarns 32, 34, 36–37, 40, 88, 122

Yamashita, Gigi 173, 200, 202
Yarn Geek Fibers 80, 201
Yarn Hollow 201
Yarn Marm 201
Yarnival 83
Yarns and Storys 201–2
YouTube 34

Acknowledgments

Thanks to God for everything, and thanks to my parents Mark and Cindy Dunagan for the work ethic they instilled in me and the education they gave me at home. Thanks to my husband Brian for making it possible—from cleaning the kitchen while I wrote, to designing and building a spinning wheel. You're my hero. And thanks to our surprise baby for making that first trimester so easy; it would have been difficult to write all this in the bathroom.

Thanks to Sarah Robbins for feeding me and letting me spend the night so we could get all the photography done. Thanks to all my fiber artist friends who inspired and challenged me to think outside the box. Thanks to Robyn Story for proofreading when my pregnancy brain made writing a challenge. Thanks to Jacey Boggs for being so open about the journey of authorship. Thanks to Lexi Boeger for all your encouragement and praise—you gave me the courage to put myself out there. Thanks to Esther Rodgers for sharing your knowledge, and to Sayra Adams for those dyeing techniques I couldn't figure out. It has been awesome having all of you on this project. Thanks to Heather Lightbody, Lisa Renee McKenzie, Lindsey Dobbs, and April Starr for your friendship and encouragement.

Thanks to everyone who contributed to this project. Thanks to all my fans who dyed fiber for me at the last minute, and shipped yarns from around the world. Thanks to the family farms, whose owners spend so much time and effort raising those fleeces we love to play with. Thanks to all my blog readers and YouTube viewers. Thanks to the Fiber Artists & Yarn Spinners Group on Facebook for being so helpful. Thanks too to my team at RotoVision for challenging me to do better than I ever imagined. It has been an incredible journey and I owe all of you a hug.

I hope you enjoy this book.

Boom goes the dynamite. Buddy, you owe me ten bucks.

Ashley Martineau
Neauveau Fiber Arts
Blog: www.handspunartyarn.com
Shop: www.shopneauveau.com